DRC

NAKED IN PARADISE

&

OTHER ESSAYS

REVISED EDITION

DAVID BAKISH

LADYBUG PRESS

Ladybug Press

Inquiries and Book Orders should be addressed to:

Great Writers Media
Email: info@greatwritersmedia.com
Phone: 877-556-0487

Library of Congress Control Number: 2023921240

ISBN: 979-8-89175-031-9 (sc)
ISBN: 979-8-89175-032-6 (ebk)

For
Linda

PREFACE

This is my second self-published book after three others placed with regular firms—*Richard Wright* (Ungar); *Afro-American Fiction, 1853-1976*, with co-author Edward Margolies (Gale Research); *Jimmy Durante: His Show Business Career* (McFarland).

I knew that my fourth book, a memoir, would not draw a publisher in what would have been a fruitless search and waste of time. *Zero to Seventy-Five in 30 Snapshots* was edited and formatted by my wife, Linda, who among other jobs had done some freelance editing for Scholastic Books. The resulting book 265-pages showed a professional touch in formatting the text and skillful placing of 30 photos. With a cherubic black and white photo of the author at age four as a cover and a color back cover of a mustached professor in his thirties, the book was registered with the Library of Congress and printed on demand by CreateSpace, a subsidiary of Amazon, and listed on Amazon.com but had no other publicity. Complimentary copies drew mostly silence or an unexplained "WOW!" from startled friends and silence from family.

Linda passed away from breast cancer complicated by progressive multiple sclerosis. Her long illness and death had me spending all my time trying to meet her needs as she struggled with unrelenting pain. My mind went into a deep depression in the precious time before and after she died.

As Thanksgiving 2019 approached my mind awoke from the depths to resume work on this, my fifth book. The book was entitled *Drowning Naked in Paradise & Other Essays*. It had more humor and no photographs aside from the front and back covers. The essays on the whole where much shorter than in the previous book and can be read independent of each other.

Some pieces were written as part of my participation in a writers group led by Ruth Lehrer, published writer and neighbor. I am grateful to members for their constructive criticism in what were bi-weekly sessions. I also want to thank Michael Greene, my MLS therapist, chosen for me by my wife as she researched the internet on her death bed. He helped with formatting and much more, including emotional support. Important encouragement and kindness were shown me by good friends: Rabbi Sidney and Ruth Solomon, Jacqueline and Aron Weinbach, Jackie Friedland (in Israel), Raizie Lutwak, Susan Cutter, Naomi Joy Greshman, Lynn Silverman May, and Fernando Giordano (moved from New York to New Orleans)..

This is a revision of *Drowning Naked...*

CONTENTS

1

Self-Publishing

I've wanted to write my autobiography for as long as I can remember, and completed the first of a number of attempts while I was still in high school.

Was there anything so extraordinary about my life that I felt the need, even as a child, to tell my story? Not really. But if you stop and think about it, you too may come to feel that we all have a story to tell, something unique and worth the effort to recount and preserve.

Was it Socrates who said that the unexamined life was not worth living? What better way to perform that examination, to take stock, and make sense out of the experiences that comprise our days on this earth?

"It is only in the narrative mode," the renowned psychologist Jerome Bruner tells us, "that one can construct an identity....Facts never exist out of context."

My own life began in New York City in 1937, but its setting soon shifted to small town northeastern Pennsylvania. My parents, Sephardic Jewish immigrants from Bulgaria, moved our family to a predominantly white, Protestant, middle American setting where they established a small factory and worked hard to succeed and raise their two children well. This meeting of cultures generated many contradictions, some of which still puzzle me today, but I was privileged to have the benefits of both worlds, and to find my own, very personal, path through life. Ultimately, I came back to New York to work and finally to marry in my 50s. I don't know that there is anything particularly instructive about my story, but it's been a life—my life—and writing it has made it more vivid and meaningful to me.

How many of us have lives distinctive enough to interest Oxford University Press, Random House, or Simon & Schuster? It must be a truly extraordinary story, often authored by a well-known personality possessing mass appeal, in order to merit such attention. I can envision a pile of rejection letters all stating your book is "not commercially viable."

What are we to do with all the stories we want to share? The self-publishing phenomenon can speak to this need. Increasingly today, writers are turning to self-publishing rather than struggle through years of daunting frustration trying to interest a trade publisher.

I produced three books over the years, all works of scholarship, the first two with contract in hand before beginning the project. One was a monograph on the expatriate African-American author Richard Wright, part of a series on modern writers. A second was a library reference work done with coauthor Edward Margolies, on African-American fiction 1853-1976. The third, a thoroughly documented study of the early show business personality Jimmy Durante, reached an enthusiastic publisher that specialized in this kind of material, but not before I spun my wheels in frustration sending the manuscript to inappropriate and uninterested companies.

Retired after years of teaching at Medgar Evers College, a branch of the City University of New York, I've had the time to write about some of the most meaningful experiences in my life so far, good and bad, happy and sad. This would be not so much a full autobiography but a selective memoir, skipping over less interesting aspects of my life. The memoir would also skip over elements too personal to be shared in public, more properly good material for a novel that stretches and embroiders the truth creatively for dramatic, storytelling effect.

I decided not to waste my time looking for a trade publisher. After investigating a number of self-publishing options, I chose CreateSpace, an affiliate of Amazon.com, and while their service has not been perfect, it has been adequate and affordable. They provided traditional print and eBook formats, a Library of Congress ISBN number, a copyright in my name, and an Amazon.com listing, plus other services if I was willing to pay for them. On paper, royalties sounded hefty in comparison with those paid by trade publishers and it can be an exciting experience to be part of the creative process of designing your book, but publicity is the missing ingredient (and so no royalties to speak of). Still, the author got to tell his story for his still-living friends, family and those few others who might find an interesting time capsule that recalls much that once was and is no more.

My memoir was entitled *Zero to Seventy-Five in 30 Snapshots*. It was actually fun writing and rewriting the thirty segments, or snapshots, with, coincidentally, thirty photographs. After the book appeared, I belatedly caught a few factual errors and still fewer misspellings despite careful proofreading. The second printing corrected such errors as misstating the publication for which my boyhood friend Art Cooper served as editor before taking over *GQ* magazine. It was *Family Weekly*, not *Family Circle*. My wonderful landlady in Delaware was from Ireland, not Scotland. Still, I missed naming the correct show business book that beat out mine on Jimmy Durante for an award: it was about Tommy Dorsey, not Jimmy Dorsey. These missteps notwithstanding, those friends and others who took the time to give feedback thought the book was well-written, candid, and even courageous in what it revealed.

Recently I was part of a writing group whose leader stressed brevity and the subjects all related to personal experience, no fiction. My second collection of essays, again self-published, much shorter than the first, is entitled *Drowning Naked in Paradise & Other Essays*. After the title piece the others are in no special order. Several aim for a touch of humor. The reader can pick any one without missing any connecting link.

The earlier edition of this book (Newman Springs, 2020) contained many misplaced commas, not my doing, that I did not catch before the printing. I guess this was a negative aspect of self-publishing.

2

Early Interest in Writing

When I was in high school the local chapter of Hadassah, the Jewish women's group, ran a contest. The topic for a poem was to be any Biblical story. I chose Moses. My brilliant friend, Hans, when told what first prize was, a big box of Barton's chocolates, asked if he could co-write the poem for half the chocolates if the poem won.

Rhyming was fun. "Moses" won first prize. We split the candy, my giving Hans his choice of which pieces he wanted from the box. I guess this was really cheating, the first and only time I took credit for work not entirely my own.

A year or two later I wrote an essay on the topic "I Speak for Democracy." The American Legion awarded first, second, and third place prizes. First prize was a check. A girl won that. The second place winner was given the choice of two 10" LPs, a recording of Ray Anthony's big band or vocals by Nat King Cole. He chose Ray Anthony. The principal then called me to the stage and joked that I had no choice but to accept the Nat King Cole LP. That's what I would have chosen anyway. The students in the auditorium laughed. That was okay with me: I loved making people laugh.

My twelfth grade teacher was in her last year before retiring. Harriet Kline was the most inspiring of teachers. She taught an awareness of the multiple styles of excellent writers through the centuries of British and American literature. What I remember most were the essays of Elizabethan author Sir Francis Bacon and the opening passage of Charles Dickens' novel *A Tale of Two Cities*. Doing what Mrs. Kline called "aping" another writer's style, I wrote an essay "On Scouting" in Bacon's style. I got an A+. What I most admired in Dickens' style was his parallel structure:

> It was the best of times, it was the worst of times, it was the age of wisdom, it was the age of foolishness, it was the epoch of belief, it was the epoch of incredulity, it was the season of Light, it was the season of Darkness, it was the spring of hope, it was the winter of despair, we had everything before us, we had nothing before us, we were all going to Heaven, we were all going direct the other way—in short, the period was so far like the present period, that some of its noisiest authorities insisted on its being received, for good or for evil, in the superlative degree of comparison only.

Strunk and White, in their influential small booklet, *The Elements of Style*, advocate short sentences. It's impressive mastery of the English language to have one sentence comprised of a long series of complete thoughts without losing control or producing unintended fragments and comma splices.

Mrs. Kline thought I was the best writer in her 1954-55 classes and wanted me to be given an award at graduation but was told by the administration that there was no such award. I settled for being inducted into the National Honor Society and the National Thespian Society, the latter despite my weak acting and directing skills.

One of the essays I wrote for Mrs. Kline was a first stab at an autobiography. It was largely about my parents' hard struggle as immigrants to this country, land of opportunity. She gave the essay an A+.

The literary highpoint of that senior year was reciting and acting out the witches scene from Shakespeare's *Macbeth*.

After that year I never tried to copy any of the many great writers I would come to admire, but my appreciation grew for both luxurious, extensive, descriptive work and more concise, laconic, muscular work. In classical American literature Hawthorne, Melville, Henry James, and Faulkner might be at one pole, F. Scott Fitzgerald, Hemingway, and J.D. Salinger at the other pole.

3

Superman

I would venture to guess that many of us old-timers, when we were young whippersnappers, imagined all the things we wanted to be when we grew up. Sure, some kids already knew what they wanted to be: doctors, lawyers, nurses, teachers, professional athletes, or just anybody rich. Some of us boys growing up in the 1940s idolized cowboys killing Indians, now so politically incorrect. Today I might root for the Indians. Cops catching hardened criminals, though we might have admired the moxie of some wily gangsters. Sharpshooting American soldiers mowing down Japs and Nazis, clearly evil people for whom none of us would have felt any sympathy. I imagined I could be like the comic strip character Clark Kent, a bumbling, awkward guy like me, magically transforming into the awesomely powerful flying machine known as Superman, a comic book invention of two Jewish writers, *nebbishes* with vivid imagination.

Well into adulthood I had dreams that I *was* Superman. The catch, however, was that my dreams turned into nightmares. I would fight off two or three bad guys, but out of nowhere they were joined by a horde of others all jumping on me. I would then try to fly off a nearby cliff but, upon launching my muscular body into the air, my red cape failed. I crashed and all the bad guys were again on top of me. When I woke up in a cold sweat, I was relieved to be alive and once again the very ordinary Clark Kent.

In real life my greatest skills lay in my writing ability. I dreamt I would one day write the great American novel or a work of non-fiction that the literary world would welcome and award me some measure of fame. Although that never happened, I was recognized in a very modest way for my research and books on the black American author Richard Wright and the popular culture singing comedian Jimmy Durante. One was dead serious about the social problem of racism; the other was a nonpolitical master of raucous humor. Still, the image of Superman continued to have its allure.

Superman sought to protect the innocent from those who would perform evil acts. He was, for me, a one-man army when conventional forces failed. Sometimes evil appeared insidiously clever and more exciting than good, but unlike in the real world, in Superman's world evil forces always lost. I hoped in some small way I could do good, even if more like Clark Kent than Superman. After all, Clark Kent was a newspaper reporter, a writer like me.

4

Something I Never Told Anyone Before

In *The Wiz*, the excellent Broadway musical reworking of the classic film *The Wizard of Oz*, there's a number that piles up negatives in a very effective way of saying "NO!": "Don't Nobody Bring Me No Bad News." Well, I could say "Don't nobody never ask me to do nothing that nobody don't need to know."

If I'm asked to reveal a deeply buried secret, I'd better lie. If there's something I don't want known, there probably is a good reason, so why should I jump into hot water now and get scalded? Torture me and I'll make up the most creative lie, like I was a friend of E.T. and came with him from another planet but stayed when he returned home.

I could say that in the most recent of several reincarnations I was Rin Tin Tin, courageous German Shepherd silent film movie star, not likely some human great like Aristotle or Napoleon, nor a villain like Rasputin or Benedict Arnold, but maybe an insignificant street sweeper in Pompeii before Mount Vesuvius demolished the city in 79 A.D. If I'm in line for still another reincarnation, I'd like to request of the Powers That Be that I'll be allowed to rest in my grave.

My spirit is exhausted from inhabiting so many bodies of men and dogs, plus, who knows, even a turtle or a sheep.

The truth, if you really must have the truth, something I never told anyone before, is that I'm transgender and born in Reykjavik to Icelandic parents who disowned me after settling in Fargo, North Dakota.

5

Naked, Or Nude

My father, Marco, as a bachelor took artful black and white photographs, many of lightning strikes across the summer sky, some of individual flowers, some of trips with friends to Niagara Falls and the Catskill Mountains. The best of these he mounted in a loose-leaf scrapbook on black pages and poetic descriptions in white ink. When he was courting my mother, he set up a timer so he could join her in "love photos." These too found their way into his scrapbook, with comments like "love calling."

When I was in high school I looked through his collection, surprised to see that he also included photos of Baby David. Then life got too complicated for my father and he threw out photography equipment like paper stock and chemicals, putting his camera in a closet unused and forgotten. Included in the discontinued scrapbook were several photos of Baby David getting a sponge bath in a bassinet from Mother Rose. One had my father's white ink remark, "I smoke my pipe." I had a little pipe that blew bubbles. Two other photos showed me in that bassinet in completely innocent, even adorable, nudity. As a self-conscious teenager I was embarrassed by a tiny penis preserved there for "all the world" to see, as though once I became famous some tabloid newspaper or magazine would publish such an

Italian Renaissance-like chubby cherub. Abject humiliation? Photo Shop had not yet been invented to doctor the photos with fig leaves or a tiny bikini. Surreptitiously I destroyed the prints, hoping my father had not kept any negatives.

I cannot recall ever seeing my mother or my father naked and if I had I would have been as embarrassed as catching them having sex—and that never happened either. I didn't even peek at my mother's breastfeeding my sister, born seven years after me, and of course I have no memory of my own breastfeeding. My mother did invite me to feel her swollen belly when my sister was kicking furiously shortly before being born.

My teenage years in the Boy Scouts were as innocent as can be. I wasn't even sure how babies were made until I sent away for a book that arrived in a plain brown wrapper. Not Dr. Spock but some 19th century writer, maybe Paolo Mantegazza, whose Italian work was translated into English except for explicit sexual passages given in Latin, like something to be worked at, decoded. Also my aunt, my father's sister, passed along a scary and outdated sex manual, not of how to do "it," but all the venereal diseases you could get from sex outside marriage, illustrated by drawings of pockmarked degenerates. I was the next in line to get the family book that warned not to do anything stupid or my penis would fall off.

When I had passed all the merit badges necessary to achieve the exulted rank of Eagle Scout except Lifesaving, I had run out of time with repeated failures at the Boy Scout summer camp and went to a neighboring town that had a YMCA with an indoor swimming pool and an instructor who could test my water skills. What I didn't know until I arrived there with my swim trunks was that the rules of that particular YMCA required nude swimming. Why? To keep the pool free of lint. My shock and chagrin at the realization that I had to swim naked and show that I could "rescue" this adult male who was also naked motivated me to pass the test on my first try. Using the cross-chest carry I towed "the victim" from the middle of the deep end to the edge of the pool.

To my mind at that time, "nude" meant Renoir; "naked" was unwanted exposure of my body, causing excruciating embarrassment.

Years later I would equate "naked" with welcome sexual excitement except on those few occasions when I visited nudist colonies and had to repress sexual feelings.

At my Bucknell University fraternity some of the brothers challenged a skinny music major to walk across 7th Street to the laundromat naked, put quarters in the soda machine and walk back across the street. The catch was that there was a woman there doing her laundry. If Skinny could successfully accomplish this without "chickening out," he would win the jackpot the other guys put together. He did it. I would not have had the guts.

In the 1950s sex seemed as remote in college as in high school. I never had any sexual experience in those years with any coed. Women were required to be in their segregated dorms, under a curfew of 10 p.m., later on weekends. But no matter. I could have had a date out until 4 a.m. and still not be able to score anything more than a less than passionate kiss. Forget getting naked or even unsnapping a brassiere.

A college friend during my graduate studies at Bucknell took me to the home of his very rich neighbor in North Jersey. At the shallow end of an elegantly designed outdoor pool she had had the architect create a statue of her in a very sensuous nude pose. As I stood admiring the statue I overheard one of the narcissistic woman's friends remark to the other, "This boy has a very handsome physique." I was proud to look good in skimpy swim trunks. Nothing more materialized, just a slightly elevated ego.

Sometime in my twenties I saw ads for nudist colonies in New Jersey inviting both nudists and neophyte curiosity seekers, the ads proclaiming how healthful nudism was. I wrote to the box numbers given and took a Greyhound bus to the first of three colonies I eventually visited. It was called Camp Goodland, near Hackettstown. Another young man about my age happened to be on the bus and we arrived at the same time. Before we were given the run of the property a stern-faced woman met us in the main office. "Gentlemen, welcome to Camp Goodland. Is this your first experience with a nudist colony?" We assured her it was. "You will find that nudism is the most natural thing, healthy for mind and body. For the first half hour that you are here I want each of you to carry a towel to cover

21

up. After that you should have no problem." While I remember the woman's introductory comments, I don't remember whether she was nude or fully dressed. Strange, right?

Walking around the grounds I saw naked men, some with great physiques, others with fat, hairy breasts and sagging stomachs, dangling testicles and not one erection. Some of the women, both young and old, were in good condition, very attractive for their years, others with double and triple stomachs and breasts hanging to their waists. No one seemed concerned. About a dozen were engaged in what I learned was the unofficial nudists' chief sport, volleyball. I joined in, and in the heat of competition got over any self-consciousness and was confident enough to drop the towel which I had wrapped around my waist. The young man who arrived with me on the bus, however, continued to have erection problems, angering one older male nudist who complained to me. "What is it with your friend, walking around with a full valise?" I replied, "He's not my friend, just a stranger who arrived on the bus with me. I haven't noticed that he's carrying any baggage."

Later in the day I played my first set of tennis in the nude on the only clay court. My only concern was that the court was not well maintained and black ants were walking everywhere.

Both regular members and newcomers were told to assemble for dinner, dressed for the meal, and later dancing. My eye earlier in the afternoon had wondered to a very attractive young woman about seventeen working as a waitress. Her mother was one of the women with a double stomach and had raised her daughter as a nudist but as Carol reached puberty she felt self-conscious and would only accompany her mother if she could be fully dressed. After dinner and dancing most of the group piled into cars, drove into town to enjoy the local bowling alley.

Families stayed in bungalows for the weekend or the entire week. I was given my own quarters for the night. From what I could see, there was no sex, just happy, healthy nudism divorced from sex. I thought it was strange that of all the women in the nude, including some very attractive people, I was drawn to a teenager who was fully clothed. The attraction in fact was so strong that I got her address in New York City and later invited her to be my guest at a Bucknell fraternity party. No one at Bucknell knew she had been a nudist and I never got to see her naked. She graduated high school and went to the University of Cincinnati to study architecture and after one last letter we lost contact with each other. The year I guess was 1960 and I was working on my Master's Degree.

This nudist experience felt surprisingly liberating though I left the camp with some uncomfortable sunburn on body parts that had never been exposed to the sun. A man who lived in Hazelton, Pennsylvania drove me in his MG sports car as far as he was going and I took a bus the rest of the way home.

The second nudist colony I visited was Sunny Rest Lodge, in the Pocono Mountains near Palmerton, Pennsylvania, in the late 1960s when I was living in Trenton, New Jersey, and the third at Sunshine Park, Cape Mays Landing in South Jersey, soon after I moved to New York City in 1971. I remember nothing about the Pocono resort and my only recollection about the Mays Landing location was swimming in the Great Egg Harbor River and playing nude tennis with the famous journalist Gay Talese as my partner. Wearing only tennis sneakers on a hot, humid summer day, I felt the macadam surface radiate extra heat to the point that I asked, "Does anyone mind if I put my shirt back on?" Perspiring a bit less, I held up my end well enough for us to win. I knew that my good tennis partner was a well-known journalist but not that through this time frame, the 1970s, he was researching a new book *Thy Neighbor's Wife* (1981), studying the sexual activities of Americans before AIDS. Did he find sex at Sunshine Park? I don't know. I certainly did not.

Only once more did I ever return to any nudist colonies. In the late 1970s I convinced my girlfriend, and another couple to visit Camp Goodland. There was no nervousness but a major thunderstorm hit in midafternoon and we had to pack it in after a short time at the pool. The place looked seedy, not as well-maintained as my first time there, and clearly not enough tennis players to warrant rebuilding the decaying tennis court. The black ants still ruled, the wood holding up the chicken wire enclosure was thoroughly rotten, and the torn net sagged so much no one was likely to double fault on a serve.

Twice I went nude swimming in ocean waters, once on Gay Head, a beautiful beach on Martha's Vineyard, with my girlfriend and a black couple who got us an inexpensive week in a basement apartment of their friends in the hamlet of Oak Bluff, a historic black community. The four of us stripped off our bathing suits and enjoyed the beach and water all to ourselves. The other time was at a crowded nude beach on the Greek island of Mykonos.

6

Drowning Naked in Paradise

In 1979, at the age of forty-two, I went nude ocean swimming in what struck me as paradise. I was out of shape from insufficent excercise and had put on some weight, but not so much as to be embarrassed by my less than svelte figure.

Traveling alone from Paris to the Greek isles by train and boat, my French girlfriend too busy to accompany me, I befriended three young Japanese tourists. Hiroshi was a worker at a car plant, and the two women, whose names I forgot, were on break from their studies in Paris. Although all three were very agreeable, when they chose to speak Japanese I was lost. The women and I could converse in French but Hiroshi knew only his native language.

Together the four of us took a boat from Athens' port of Piraeus to the beautiful island of Mykonos, in the crystal clear Aegean Sea. Hiroshi and I slept in a clean, simple and inexpensive rooming house run by a woman who met our incoming boat, rather than seeking out an expensive hotel room. One day the two young women went off on their own and I persuaded Hiroshi to stick with me as I sought transportation to what was reportedly a famous nude beach. What he understood of what I was saying was never clear. All the English he knew came from a Japanese-English phrase book.

When the owner of a small motorboat took us to a nude beach the tourists called Paradise, Hiroshi was surprised to find buck naked people, and I was surprised to find only men. "Where are all the women?" I asked the skipper, who understood English. "Oh, I see two men so I think they want the homosexual beach. There is another beach with men and women. My mistake. I take you there."

Now on what tourists nicknamed Super Paradise I saw luscious blonde nude women, Scandinavians taking off their string bikinis and getting full-body tans to take back to cold northern countries. All the men and women I saw were physically fit, no double stomachs or sagging breasts. I was too overcome by all this beauty to approach any one of them, as though each nude were a sculpture in the Louvre back in Paris, Venus de Milos, but with added arms, torso, and legs. In any case, there were two of us who under other circumstances might have asked two beauties to join us, risking rejection, but what was I to do with a shy friend who spoke only Japanese?

We found a spot for our towels, and Hiroshi seemed very puzzled now but did not know how to ask, "Where am I and why all the people with no clothes?" This would have been more than his phrase book could have handled. He sat on his towel staring at the sand, afraid to look up or even to take his polo shirt off, much less his trunks. I signaled that I was going into the water, using improvised sign language, hands making swimming motions. He nodded and used the word that seems to be international, "okay."

I swam out past the anchored yachts, enjoying the quiet lapping of clear water, only to discover that there was an undertow. As I tried to return to shore I was silently, insistently, carried further away. Had I come to this idyllic, romantic island, to a beach called Super Paradise, only to drown? And completely naked? With a Japanese friend who did not even know my last name? And no lifeguards?

I felt the sharp edge of fear and thought of calling out to someone on a nearby yacht for help, but how would that work? "Help! Help! I'm drowning! So sorry to interrupt your cocktail hour. I hope you don't mind having a naked man on your boat. Please excuse me for not being a beautiful young woman or a mermaid."

My mind began working hard to calm me down. "Look, you're a macho man, like that song from the Village People that Club Med likes to play at beach parties together with 'Y.M.C.A.' And you have Boy Scout swimming and lifesaving merit badges. Lifesaving passed at a YMCA, in the nude."

I felt the pleasant softness of the water gently caressing me.

"Yeah?," I answered myself, "but I was in much better shape then."

Floating on my back, gathering my strength, I appreciated the sun, high in the midday sky, warm and bright.

"Of course, but you still have the skills, like riding a bike."

A few seagulls glided silently by. Calm began to conquer fear.

"Yeah, I *do* remember what I learned so many years ago: swim parallel to the beach, work your way slowly inward, float on your back to rest when you get tired. You're okay. This is terrific exercise."

The beach was now within reach, as if its closeness had been willed by my still-calm brain.

As I staggered onto the beach like a shipwreck survivor, dazed from the struggle and nearsighted without my glasses, I reached the blur that I recognized as Hiroshi. Looking in his phrase book, he asked, "Good time?" Breathing hard I could only say "Okay," as I dropped onto my sandy towel. I closed my eyes to the sky, exhausted, but not too tired to imagine folding my arms around one of the gorgeous women, with no daylight between our bodies.

7

Amnesia Through Age Five,
and Sitting Still

Strange for someone with an almost photographic memory for many people's faces and events in a life that so far has carried me within striking distance of age ninety, but I have no memory at all of the first five years of my life. Oh sure, I was told about multiple events multiple times by my mother, and I looked at early photographs my father took before he stopped thinking I was cute and adorable, but the first thing I actual remember was the first day of kindergarden at the Ben Franklin Normal School far from our house. Betty Moser wet her pants and, in tears, was taken home by her mother. The rest of the year is a blank.

I do remember a few events of the first grade at the nearby Fifth Street Elementary School, primarily because Miss Krauss was the only Jewish teacher and reported home to my mother that I had trouble sitting still. She had me sharpening large batches of pencils, and maybe this was the year when I was sent out to the very rudimentary, gravel-covered playground to pick up candy wrappers and other garbage, wielding a long stick with a nail on the end. I also remember being home in bed with the measles and Miss Krauss—

her first name was Sarah—visiting me, maybe giving me a coloring book, but I'm not sure of that. Her visit struck me as an honor, my teacher coming to my house, the only time that ever happened, ever.

Second grade passed like a blur. I could recall only the teacher's name, a Miss or Mrs. Gorey. I'm not even sure I got the name correct, and I don't think I ever knew her first name. Most teachers did not give out their first names, like that was some kind of dark secret. And her face is also a blur. I have no memory of any class projects, anything I learned, or any discipline problems I might have created. Nothing.

My memory started to focus more clearly in the third grade. In the classroom of Mrs. Bundens—I later discovered her first name was Victoria—I remember being assigned a part in a play and missing one rehearsal because that school day my father was driving my family back from New York City where we visited my mother's two sisters, Clara and Martha. It was a boring and exhausting four and a half hour trip, long before the interstate highway system had been built, with Route 80 significantly shortening the travel time. Sitting on a steel railing at the edge of the school property, I stared into the distant window of my first floor classroom. My watch told me the school day was almost ending. Eagle-eyed Mrs. Bundens saw me and, opening the window, called out, "David, come in, we're rehearsing the play. We can use you." I enjoyed being the focus of positive attention as an actor, much better than forced to sit still in my assigned seat. Most of all, however, I recall being kept after school another day for misbehaving. I stubbornly refused to apologize, like the bull-headed Taurus that I was. I wore down the teacher until she let me go home without an apology. She whacked other boys on the butt for various misbehavior but I was spared that indignity. I wondered how girls in the class could sit still and avoid punishment. Maybe girls were given less freedom to act out while, as the saying goes, "boys will be boys," meaning rambunctious and hard to control.

8

Two Wooden Candlestick Holders

In my living room, on a shelf between the TV and the window, I keep two wooden candlestick holders. A classmate skilled in woodworking made them from the ornate and well-worn bannister that led from our elementary school's first floor, with its six classrooms, grades one, two, and three, to the second floor's grades four through six. Mementoes were salvaged when the building was demolished after sitting lonely and empty for many years.

The old place had no gymnasium, library, lunch room, nurse's room, or faculty lounge, in fact, no amenities. There was a backroom for the principal, the only male teacher, where he could paddle misbehaving students sent to him for firm correction. His own sixth grade class would await his return, listening through a closed door to the whacks and screams.

In the closing years of World War II the class that collected the most tin cans and scrap metal to help the war effort got its name on a huge banner that hung at the top of the staircase.

Although the likelihood of a German or Japanese plane attacking a school in a small northeastern Pennsylvania town was remote at best, our principal held regularly scheduled air raids. At the sound of alarm bells, teachers lined us up by twos and led us down another less ornate staircase into the asbestos-covered jumble of heating and water pipes in the cellar. When the same bells sounded the "all clear," we were marched back up the many stairs to refocus on the day's studies.

I was glad for any interruption to break up the boredom of having to sit still for some dumb, uninteresting lesson, putting on the act of paying attention. To pass the time I would doodle, drawing three-dimensional box houses with sharply peaked roofs, or intricately fold a sheet of paper to make a "cootie" catcher that could nip the hair of the student in front of me, hopefully without the no-nonsense, humorless teacher seeing what I was doing.

For those curious, I never got paddled in grade school—just punished in many other ways, like being denied recess when the others got to go out and play. In junior high school an industrial arts teacher, an emaciated but sinewy fundamentalist Christian, wacked me with both his own woodworked paddle and a breadboard I was supposed to finish to take home to my mother. Spring baseball fever had me simulating a home run swing with a defective metal file. Its wood handle remained in my hand like the knob of a broken bat while the file flew through the air to hit another student on the back of his head. Thankfully, he was not hurt. I didn't mind too much being punished, though I felt the instructor should have kept his equipment in better, safe, condition.

Two wooden candlestick holders sitting on a shelf bring back many memories.

9

A Most Flamboyant
Teacher (Or Two)

M t. Pleasant High School in suburban Wilmington, Delaware was in the 1960s a very fine school, producing many Merit Scholars and other students who went on to good colleges and solid careers. It was here that I had my very first full-time position teaching 10th grade English.

Most of the faculty were colorful in the extreme. Three moonlighted at a racetrack and, despite their education, sounded like hoodlums from the crap game depicted in Frank Loesser's Broadway musical *Guys and Dolls*. Inspired by Damon Runyon's newspaper reportage, the show's book depicted the gamblers' efforts to find a place safe from police raids and a Salvation Army doll seeking to save sinners' souls.

Three or more faculty were gays whose sexual lives were out of view in the closet, two married and with children. The most flamboyant ran an opera club and took students to Philadelphia's Academy of Music and once or twice to New York's Metropolitan Opera. His boyfriend sometimes joined the group but never his wife. I often joined in, but in three years of teaching in that high school never met his wife except at their home once to exchange hellos.

At opera performances all nearby heads turned to Mr. Giamboy to protest his loud gunshot-like clapping after every aria. After the final curtain fell, we were herded backstage with photos in our hands, with hopes of getting autographs while Mr. Giamboy gushed over a few words with the stars. An 11th grade teacher, Giamboy was very popular with his students, but jealous of the even greater popularity and even greater flamboyance of a 10th grade English teacher.

Ken Schomborg was tall, gaunt almost to the point of resembling a cadaver or Holocaust survivor. There was talk that he was a survivor of the Bataan death march of American prisoners, cruelly perpetrated by the Japanese in World War II. When he spoke his voice came out a mellow bass and his deeply set eyes gleamed. He could merely say "Hello" to his students and make that one word sound significant, fraught with deep meaning. He was a Don Quixote, an idealist who could make you believe anything was possible.

Ken's home was a modest and sparsely furnished apartment. It was directly across the hall from his closest friend, Helen Merrill, an excellent but soft-spoken and non-flamboyant 11th grade English teacher who got that grade's students not assigned to Giamboy. The long and close relationship between Ken and Helen, I speculated, was loving but probably platonic.

After the long and tiring school day was over, I would often drag my exhausted body to Schomborg's apartment, sit on a cushion on the hardwood floor of the mostly unfurnished living room and try to absorb a master's philosophy of life flowing as a fountain from an alcoholic but brilliant teacher who sat on a cushion facing me from across the room. When the oversize glass of whisky, diluted only by a couple of ice cubes, began to cloud my mind so I could absorb no more words of wisdom, I concluded it was time to leave.

Both of these terrific teachers are now dead but they live on in the many students they inspired. And in me. Passed along to a new generation was their love of learning for its own sake, not for money that might or might not come from careers. I could not match the brilliance of either one, but I would try to be a good teacher, with just a touch of flamboyance.

10

What If?

You could go on and on and on with speculation of how things might have worked out—for you, for the country, for the world—if some decision had been made or not made.

On a personal level, I often imagine what might have gone wrong in driving my father's new 1955 automatic shift V-8 engine Plymouth at its speedometer's top number, 120 miles per hour. As a senior in high school I had the brilliant idea of testing out the car on a clear, as-yet-unopened new highway with my friend John as passenger and witness. What if a farmer's tractor had suddenly crossed the road? What if the tires had overheated and blown out? Would the car have flipped over? What if without seat belts my passenger and I had been thrown through the windshield? Would I be here to write about my teenage recklessness? I felt the steering wheel shake as the car passed 100 mph and strained to reach 120. After this adventure my mind told me I would never want to be a NASCAR driver. The fastest I ever drove after that was 90 mph on an open highway in the West, where the speed limit was 75 mph. Road safety has gotten better over these many years since the 1950s, the era of James Dean (the young actor who famously died in a car crash): seat belts, anti lock brakes, and airbags. Still, too many young male drivers remain fearlessly reckless, defying death.

What if when I was teaching high school in Wilmington, Delaware in the early 1960s, I had married the daughter of one of Delaware's most prominent and richest Jewish families? Her family liked me. I said no. Would I ever have had the time, desire and energy to complete a Ph.D., publish books, and spend a career teaching college in the heart of New York City? Or would I have worked for her family? Would we have had children? Would we eventually divorce or live happily ever after? After fifty years I ran across her photo through Google online and she looked hardly changed. Was this a recent photo? What was her life like? Healthy and happy, or not?

What if Amherst College, an excellent small liberal arts school in Massachusetts, had hired me as a literature professor? Would I have developed my teaching and writing skills more deeply and would I have achieved tenure and promotions? After the turmoil at Medgar Evers College, CUNY, during its first full year of operation, 1971-72, I sent my resume to Amherst and was invited to visit its campus for an interview. Jaws visibly dropped when I entered the room. The panel liked my written credentials: teaching at a predominately black college; published articles on such African-American writers as Richard Wright, Amiri Baraka (LeRoi Jones), and Chester Himes; a doctoral dissertation on Richard Wright and a subsequent book on Wright. They expected to see an African-American man. I was not offered a position. Later, and unrelated, I was invited to fill out a form that would include me in the publication of *Who's Who Among Black Americans*. I wrote back in appreciation, politely declining the honor.

On a national and international level another bunch of "What if's?" present themselves. What if the Japanese had not attacked Pearl Harbor in 1941? Would the U.S. have remained isolationist until too late to save England, and thus, all of Western Europe? And all of Asia and North Africa? Economists say the government can go for guns or butter, not both at the same time. President Franklin D. Roosevelt found that after the Japanese attack and the subsequent German declaration of war on the United States, building our war capability (guns) would lead to higher employment than any WPA program (butter) and would be a major factor in ending the Great Depression.

Again dealing with World War II, what if Nazi Germany had not broken its non-aggression pact with the Soviet Union? Would the absence or delay of a divided front have spelled victory for Germany? The consequences are too frightening to imagine, especially for someone like me, a Jew, a target for the Nazis' insane project of annihilation, genocide, wiping out every Jewish man, woman, and child on the face of the earth. As a corollary, what if Nazi Germany had developed the atomic bomb before the United States? Another horror too frightening to contemplate.

More recently, in the 1960s, what if, instead of escalating the war in Vietnam, President Lyndon B. Johnson had realized its futility and had found a way out, freeing millions if not billions of dollars for the war on poverty in our own country, while sparing the lives of thousands of American soldiers and Vietnamese civilians? In that situation the economists' view that you had to choose guns or butter was correct. Vietnam was not as vital an American interest as was saving the world from German and Japanese domination. Some statesmen, like hawkish Secretary of Defense Robert McNamara (1961-1968), believed in the domino theory, that if any country fell to Communism many others could fall. Vietnam's nationalistic pride was actually stronger than its Communist impulse, and Ho Chi Minh was a national hero to many after defeating the French.

On a less serious note, I wonder, fancifully, what if on the first date I had with the woman who would become my wife I had appeared with bird droppings on my tie and a piece of spinach hanging from my upper front teeth? And what if I told her that her jacket shoulder pads made her look like an NFL fullback? And that her phone's voice message needed rerecording? Would I have been given the opportunity to clean up my image with a second date? Would she see through the Woody Allen awkwardness to the inner me? What if her mother had taken the advice to abort the late-life pregnancy that resulted in my beautiful, smart and witty wife-to-be, Linda, being born? What would I have done without her? Nothing. I never would have known.

There are so many other what if's. What if I were born in Bulgaria instead of the United States? What if I were born a girl? What if I had been drafted into the army? What if I had finished law school and become a lawyer instead of a college professor with job security? What if I had never married? What if my wife's health had been better and we travelled more instead of being tied down with our lovable dogs? What if we had decided to have children? What if climate change were to make our planet unlivable? What if extraterrestrials were to save our planet instead of attacking it? What if Democrats and Republicans embraced each other and worked together for the common good?

11

Pet Peeves

Airports and airplanes. Remember the good old days? The excitement of embarking on a new adventure, solicitous flight attendants, hot meals? Welcome to the present. Stand on a long line to go through security, take off your shoes, put them back on, pay extra for a bit of legroom, and bring your own sandwich. Progress?

Texting on a smart phone while driving. Why worry about an accident?

Nose picking. Is anyone watching?

The F-Word. Aren't there any better descriptive adjectives and verbs?

Islamists. Intolerance, coupled with brutal sharia law and gruesome violence, all in the name of God?

Misogynists. Do women deserve enslavement or equal rights?

Pharmaceutical companies that put profit above everything else. How much profit is enough?

Unlimited contributions to political contests. Why not fix our roads, bridges and transportation with the money now wasted?

Cigarettes. Are they sexy like John Wayne and Humphrey Bogart, or just carcinogenic?

People who talk but don't listen. I remember visiting that famous nostalgia music dj Joe Franklin in his New York office. At the time, the 1970s, Joe had several phones that were not connected to each other. I witnessed him moving from one phone to another to another, saying "Hello" at each phone, all partially buried under disorganized piles of sheet music, celebrity photos, and LPs. Joe can be a great raconteur but not a great listener. There's an apocryphal story about a phone call he got from a fan. Calmly seeking the right phone, the one ringing, he is rumored to have had a conversation something like this— "Hello? Harry? Great that you called. How are you?" "Not so good. My mother just died." "Beautiful! Keep up the good work and call me again soon. Bye."

What's YOUR laundry list of pet peeves? I promise to listen.

12

Life's Metamorphoses

The black American author LeRoi Jones early in his career wrote a short poem describing the evening stars and the innocent sweetness of his young daughter, within a booklet of poems, both entitled *Preface to a Twenty-Volume Suicide Note* (1961).

Mad-hatter advice to the severely depressed from Dr. David Bakish, career English literature professor, author of an encyclopedia article on Jones, and self-proclaimed psychologist: If you actually take the time to write twenty volumes your mood may change enough that you'll forget why you even thought of suicide. At the very least you may find the motivation to continue living long enough to finish the twentieth, then commit suicide when dozens of publishers' rejection slips push you over the edge of your mental cliff. But just maybe you can have a bestseller and spend your newly rich life on yachts, private planes, and Bentley cars, or working free-of-charge with other suicidal souls.

LeRoi Jones changed his name to Amiri Baraka and his whole outlook changed and so can yours. Not that this prolific writer ever considered suicide, but he did divorce his white Jewish wife Hettie Jones—maybe because she was not radical enough or too white for his black nationalistic leanings.

You too can dump your mate, change your name and religion, even change your sex.

Roses are red, violets are blue./ You are a Muslim, I am a Jew./ When suicidal thoughts occur,/ Become a Jew and settle for the flu.

13

From Louis Armstrong to Benny Goodman

I loved jazz
And all that razz-a-ma-tazz.
Then more modern performers
Became transformers,
Smashing hipsters' cool lingo and hot chops,
Charlie Parker and Dizzy cutting dancers with be-bops.
When jazz itself got drowned by hip hop and rap,
My mind turned off what I saw as crap.
Now I'm a fossil, called a moldy fig
By youngsters whose music I don't dig.
I miss the clever lyrics of Cole Porter
And the sax of Wayne Shorter.
Oh for the music of Duke Ellington and Count Basie,
With vocals of Sarah Vaughn only slightly racy.
It may be true,
as Duke's band blew,
It don't mean a thing
If it ain't got that swing.

14

June

"June is bustin' out all over"
Wrote Oscar Hammerstein for *Carousel*,
Beautiful lyrics of nature's exuberance
Following a cold winter and a damp spring.
Children finish school and luxuriate in their freedom.
Couples embrace their wedding nuptials.
Meadows are lusciously green,
Streams gorgeously hypnotic after spring rains.
Ocean beaches warm to the anticipation of swimmers.
Mosquitoes emerge to bite and be eaten by frogs.
Birds build their nests and lay their eggs.
Families plan trips to the mountains in July's heat.
The young and healthy cry out in joy
While the old and sick remember past years
When for them June was indeed bustin' out all over.

15

Rhymes with June

I had a lot of fun with my writing group. One day our leader asked us to come up with as many words as we could think of that rhymed with "June." Here is that list compiled by the ten of us:

balloon	prune
tune	boon
ruin	cocoon
moon	maroon
typhoon	macaroon
loon	croon
octoroon	rune
goon	buffoon
platoon	saloon
coon	baboon
cartoon	pontoon
soon	macoun (type of apple)
noon	teaspoon

raccoon	tablespoon
harpoon	swoon
spittoon	afternoon
honeymoon	strewn
spoon	impugn

Add to this nonsense my jingle: I'm a buffoon/To sip tea/With a baboon.

16

My Lost Weekend

Where did the weekend go? I know I wasn't in a drunken stupor or salivating for a drink like Ray Milland in that old black and white Billy Wilder film classic *The Lost Weekend*. I know I had a blind date but I can't remember her name. I know she wasn't blind because she looked right through me and, I guess, she saw nothing. Am I transparent or too dull to inspire at least a little warmth or even animosity? If on a date you can't have a bit of animal attraction or repulsion, what good is it? Not remembering anything on a date is like receiving your FBI Freedom of Information file with every important piece of personal information redacted— you know, every page censored by big black blobs of ink—or wiping out your memory card on your smart phone before getting a new phone on which you forget to reinstall the mass of information.

I know I met her at a prearranged place—was it a coffee shop? Then we walked some street in the Village to go somewhere for something. What was it? A donut? A pack of index cards? A Baby Ruth candy bar? A pack of cigarettes for her? I don't smoke and I'm not sure if she did. I might have suggested we sit on separate benches if she lit up a cigarette. We did sit somewhere to talk, but I have no idea what we talked about. Was it the weather? Was it baseball?

Our careers? The difference between the philosophies of Plato and Aristotle? I don't even remember what she looked like. She might have even been a young man in drag for all I noticed.

As I sit at my desk on a rainy Monday morning, I know like Little Orphan Annie that the sun will come out tomorrow. Maybe after a not too stressful work week the new blind date I have scheduled for next weekend with be more memorable.

17

Onions and Orchids

In my small town Pennsylvania high school so many years ago, graduating class of 1955, a popular pastime was listing things we disliked and things we liked: spinach no, chocolate marshmallow ice cream yes. Here is a current list of my onions and orchids. It's mostly political, no ice cream.

ONIONS—PEOPLE ALIVE (known to be alive as of this writing)
Vladimir Putin. The gremlin in the Kremlin, Russia's despotic president, ex-KGB agent, sending troops into Ukraine, not to attack military target but hospitals and schools while denying such civilian targets were struck. He ordered opponents jailed, poisoned, pushed out of windows. Friendly with President Trump, both admiring and seeking total power..
Xi Jinping. Denying freedom of speech and brooking no dissent, he is President of the People's Republic of China, a threat to America's economic and military dominance. Memory of the Tiananmen Square protests and massacre (April 15, 1989) remains fresh in generations of idealistic youth.

Dictators in whatever countries they crap upon. Among them
Omar al-Bashir of Sudan, who committed Darfur geno-
cide(now held in prison); **Robert Mugabe**, president of
Zimbabwe, who ruthlessly remained in power despite
election defeats (died at age 95); **Bashar al-Assad**, president of Syria who slaughtered his own people as Saddam
Hussein had done in Iraq; **Kim Jong Un**, the crazy and
murderous dictator of North Korea.

The American Tea Party. Bent on destroying the Republican
Party by purging moderates, liberals long extinct in the
ranks. Among politicians it helped elect was **Ted Cruz**,
extremist Senator from Texas, despised by his own col-
leagues, and later as The Freedom Caucus helped elect
Donald Trump President despite his total dishonesty.

The National Rifle Association. As right wing as the Tea Party.
Their motto might as well be guns for everyone everywhere, even in bars.

George W. Bush. Former President, former alcoholic and "C"
student. Got America into unnecessary war with Iraq,
compounded by poor advice from Vice-President **Dick
Cheney** who might be best known for his insistence that
waterboarding (near drowning) was not torture.

Clarence Thomas. U.S. Supreme Court Justice. A black man
guilty of racial betrayal, lacking compassion for minori-
ties like himself and the poor. Horrible choice by the first
President Bush.

Donald J. Trump. Twice impeached former President, under
four indictments including a plot to reverse the honest
results of the 2020 election; dangerous to Democracy's
survival...

Rudy Giuliani. Radical move from 9/11 hero as mayor to lying
villain supporting Donald Trump's multiple lies; disbarred
and charged along with Trump.

Rupert Murdoch. The evil power behind **Fox News** and its
intentional right-wing political lies, motivated by greed
for more money..

Islamic extremists. Especially but not limited to ISIS, a fanatic group bey under four indictments, ond barbarism, and the more civilized but still fanatic Iranian Supreme Leader **Ayatollah Ali Khamenei.** Women without hair covering (*hajab*) are harshly punished under the Taliban; they are also forbidden to seek higher education.

Benjamin Netanyahu. With his right-wing Likud Party, comparable to the Republican Party in America, avoiding sincere peace effort by continuing to build new settlements in the West Bank.

Hamas. Their leaders in Gaza refuse to recognize Israel's right to exist, considering Israel a sty in their eye, while real peace could provide a better life for all in the region. Rockets shot at civilians in Israel don't help the chances for a peace treaty.

ORCHIDS—PEOPLE ALIVE (as of this writing)

Barack Obama. America's first black president. Gentlemanly law professor chewed up in dog-eat-dog Washington.

Hillary Clinton. One tough lady with experience during her husband's presidency and as Secretary of State in President Obama's administration. Might have made an excellent first woman president, but incredibly lost to low-life Donald Trump in 2016.

Bill Clinton. Charming and brilliant. Able to work with Republicans in his Presidency.

Charles Schumer. New York senator with unlimited energy and good ideas.

Nancy Pelosi. Skillful House Speaker working against GOP extremists.

Liz Cheney. Conservative congresswoman punished by cowardly party members for speaking the truth about President Trump.

Joe Biden. President Obama's Vice-President; later, President. Congenial despite tragic family history, doing his best to repair damage to Democracy by former President Trump..

Jimmy Carter. So-so president but angel-like organizer of home building for poor people after leaving the Presidency.

Aung San Suu Kyi. Persecuted opposition leader in Myanmar (formerly Burma). Nobel Peace Prize in 1991 for her non-violent struggle for democracy and human rights.

The 14th Dalai Lama. Tibetan Buddhist with an inspirational moral compass. Nobel Peace Prize in 1989. Exiled to India by oppressive Chinese leaders who fear democracy.

Volodymyr Zelensky. Courageous Present of Ukraine resisting Russian invasion.

Pope Francis. Refreshingly gave first priority to the poor of planet Earth and set an example for others.

Southern Poverty Law Center. From its headquarters in a former cradle of racial violence, (Birmingham, Alabama), the Center tracks America's many hate groups.

Warren Buffett. Billionaire investor with a heart. Contributor to moderate political candidates and causes.

18

Solitaire

For a guy who was a loner much of his life, at least before a late marriage at age 52, you would think I would not want to compound being alone by playing Solitaire, but that's the only indoor game I like, and that only for relaxation between other activities: reading history books or watching old black and white movies on my computer in a room separate from my ailing wife who wanted to rest, the only TV set turned off.

It's my guess that more than a few retirees like myself would prefer socializing instead of spending an evening of playing bridge. Quite often when I meet new people of a certain age, they ask, "Do you play bridge?" I know that card game is great for keeping your mind alive. Has the card I'm looking for been played yet? What signals must I give my partner to indicate we should be in three-no-trump? In my college days so long ago, I was held hostage by bridge fanatics who tied me to a chair and forced me to learn the game. Help! Can't the four of us just sit on the comfortable sofa and recliner telling stories of our more interesting life experiences? The time one of us almost drowned? How each of us met our spouses? Perhaps the more sensitive issue of why one of us got divorced? What our children and grandchildren are doing that makes us proud, or why we chose not to have children? Maybe a few clean jokes no one has heard before? Even what doctors might be good for arthritis and other ailments?

Solitaire is boring if you play the simplest forms, not some free cell version, but that's what I wanted. The games are only filler between other solitary activities. When I won a game, maybe with a personal best record-breaking score, my wide computer screen lit up with twirling cards exploding into fireworks, tumbling down a hill like a rollercoaster, rotating as a merry-go-round, or my favorite, butterflies flapping their wings and flying in all directions. That's enough excitement even with the sound turned off. (On the very next hand I might score zero points and be told "Good game!" as some game designer's perverse sense of humor.)

As a child, I loved "Spin the Bottle" to see if, despite my shyness, I could kiss a girl. As a young adult I loved any indoor game that might have turned into a sexual adventure. As a middle-age bachelor with a steady girlfriend, Aurora, I enjoyed playing backgammon. Now a senior citizen, widowed after a good marriage and no longer with my little dog near my feet, alone when my girlfriend from Brooklyn is not here to watch a movie together, I play Solitaire.

19

My Biggest High

It's certainly not drugs. It's not speeding across a remote Wyoming highway in a Maserati or Porsche. It's not hurtling up and down on a giant rollercoaster. It might, conceivably, be skydiving or bungee jumping, though I'm sure I would be too frightened to try such daredevil adventures. Driving my father's car at 120 miles per hour when as a teenager I first got my license was as much as I ever challenged death. As a senior citizen distractedly reading AARP's *Modern Maturity* reports on balding, sexual dysfunction, prostate enlargement, incontinence, facelifts, and other potentially depressing topics that I hoped would never apply to me, I try for such emotional highs as listening to the "Ode to Joy" in the fourth movement of Beethoven's 9th symphony.

My biggest high might sound trite to many, but I would say that it's watching a beautiful sunset as rapidly changing and darkening hues blend with the sounds of the ocean. Total hypnosis. If you are so inclined, you might conclude that this is one of the innumerable wonders of an exquisite, unexplainable universe.

If my wife and I had had children, our shared high might have been their birth, followed by helping them grow, get a good education, marry compatible mates, and have children of their own that we could watch and help grow. The birth of any organism may be the greatest miracle of all, especially development of the human brain. Think of it: Einstein's brain developed from a tiny sperm fertilizing a tiny egg. Few of us are Einsteins, but the chances are that when we were born, we were our parents' biggest highs of their lives. As we developed our own individual personalities, some of our parents may have had moments when they regretted having children. As Frank Sinatra might sing, that's life—highs and lows, ups and downs.

20

Mental Chatter and
My Tennis Game

(Written before an injury to my right leg made me give up my favorite sport)

Why is my tennis game so awful today? The weather is perfect: no wind, no sun, no oppressive heat or humidity. The last time I played I had to deal with strong gusts of wind. If I aimed a shot to the left corner, the wind carried the ball to the right. If I aimed at the right corner, the ball curved into the next court, far out of bounds. Somehow I found this challenge fun and I played better, maybe because I had to concentrate harder, focus better.

I was laughing then. Today I'm getting angry at my missed shots, my unforced errors. Maybe I need to relax more when I find myself not playing well. Perhaps I should experiment with a quickie meditation between games. On the changeover, walking to the other side, or between sets, I could try to make my mind blank, close my eyes, and imagine my slow sips of cold water are from a scenic mountain spring as it gurgles over small smooth rocks. The pause that refreshes might not be any carbonated soda but a brief act of mind control.

21

A Brush with Fame

The modernist artist Andy Warhol is credited with saying that in the future everyone will be famous for 15 minutes. I didn't think his multi-colored posters of Marilyn Monroe and those of Campbell soup cans would exceed 15 minutes of fame, certainly not becoming an important part of late 20th century culture, but they have.

As for me, an obscure writer-professor, my 15 minutes of fame may have come and gone when after completing my book on the career of comedian Jimmy Durante I gave a presentation to the New York Sheet Music Society at the prestigious Players Club on Gramercy Park in Manhattan on March 4, 1995. In attendance were some of Tin Pan Alley's leading composers and lyricists. You might not recognize their names but would probably know some of the songs they wrote when Tin Pan Alley was in its prime, and famous vocalists, like Frank Sinatra, put the songs across as hit records.

I was nervously excited to present material on one of the most beloved performers from the first six decades of the 20th century, not just to any audience, but to professionals who had known Durante on a personal level and loved him. To me, Jimmy was the loving, funny grandfather I never had. One of my grandfathers was an abusive, alcoholic French teacher abandoned by his wife in Bulgaria when she fled to America with her son and daughter. The other was, I understand from my mother, an honest storekeeper and good father to seven children, who died of tuberculosis in Bulgaria during World War II. I never knew either. In my mind, Durante *was* my grandfather in their absence.

Enthusiastically supplementing my anecdotes and recordings was the talented Ricky Ritzel complete with a big prosthetic nose doing material from his Durante act, *Schnozzola!*, then at the Eighty-Eights, a Greenwich Village cabaret.

Afterwards I answered questions from the full-house audience, including Ervin Drake, perhaps best known for "I Believe," made a hit by Frankie Laine, and "It Was a Very Good Year," a song Sinatra added to his repertoire. Then I sat at a table to autograph copies of my book. My wife, meanwhile, was approached in the ladies room. "Isn't it wonderful to be married to such an interesting man?" To this my Linda responded, "You should try living with him." I suppose it's a wife's duty to see that her husband doesn't develop a swell head, keeping his ego at a size that fits under a hat.

22

Brief Encounters

O ver the years I've had a number of very brief chance encounters with celebrities. Nowhere near rich or famous myself, I had no access to celebrities at cocktail parties or fundraisers, nor did I feel such encounters would have enriched my life in any meaningful way. Here are the brief encounters I have had, most of them occurring by chance in the 13 years that I lived in Manhattan, 1971-1984, but not all.

When I was in grade school I saw President Harry S Truman in 1948 on a train campaigning with a whistle stop in Bloomsburg, my hometown from the age of four. Somewhere in the blur of years that followed no other famous people passed through except some professional baseball and football scouts and players stopping at the fields of the local college, in those days still small, Bloomsburg State Teachers College. I generally was not an autograph seeker then or later but I got the signature of Philadelphia Eagles halfback Steve Van Buren on a cardboard box of pretzels. When the St. Louis Cardinals baseball team came scouting prospects I think I met Enos Slaughter. The only local sports celebrity, from nearby Ringtown, was the Cincinnati Reds outfielder Danny Litwhiler. I vaguely remember meeting him. Many years later, Art Cooper, a childhood friend from Berwick, became a reporter for *Newsweek*, head of *Family Weekly*, then very prominently head of *Gentlemen's Quarterly*, renamed *GQ*. Art, with whom I played a very incompetent version of church league basketball, had his own lunch table at the Four Seasons restaurant with celebrities like comedy writer-performer Mel Brooks. In Manhattan I did not horn in on Art's life and sought him out just once for a brief encounter.

At Bucknell University various celebrities visited to give lectures. I heard Edward R. Murrow, CBS broadcaster; B.F. Skinner, psychologist; and Margaret Mead, anthropologist. I don't remember anything any of them said, just that Murrow chain-smoked while speaking, as he did on his television news shows, Skinner talked about the stimulus-response element of his so-called "Skinner box," and Mead, whose books on Polynesian sexuality I had read on my own, sat in a women's dorm lounge eating all the pistachio nuts in a bowel on the lamp table next to her. There was some talk about illustrious alumni, author Philip Roth and the baseball and football star Christy Mathewson, for whom the football stadium was named. Oh, yes, and at a wedding reception for my Bucknell friend and his bride at the Princeton Inn I caught a glimpse of Allen Dulles, he of CIA notoriety and brother of President Eisenhower's Secretary of State John Foster Dulles, there for some other function.

After receiving my master's degree I taught English at a very good high school in Wilmington, Delaware. There I befriended another English teacher who had a passion for grand opera. Many times I went with him and the students in his opera club to the Philadelphia Academy of Music. After each thrilling performance of some Puccini or Verdi opera, Frank Giamboy handed us photographs of the opera stars, to be autographed backstage. The most memorable backstage moment for me was talking to the very warm and humorous Jewish tenor Richard Tucker. It was Valentine's Day and Mr. Tucker was showing off a gift from his wife: his new boxer shorts covered with red Valentine hearts. He autographed the photo I handed him by curving the letters "Richard Tucker" around his nose as he laughed. Other opera stars encountered over my three years teaching at the high school included Franco Corelli, Anna Moffo, Birgit Nilsson, and Joan Sutherland. Shirley Verrett, an African-American mezzo-soprano, told me she had a son named David.

In downtown Wilmington's Rodney Square, named after a signer of the Declaration of Independence, I heard President Johnson give a speech. During one of his brief pauses I shouted out one word, "PEACE!" This was my protest against the war in Vietnam. Sharpshooters on nearby buildings and plainclothes secret service agents made no move toward me and the speech continued. I guess this qualified as a brief encounter.

Fast forward to 1971 and my arrival as a 34-year-old bachelor moving into a rental apartment on West 57th Street in Manhattan. The one bedroom apartment was dreary and devoid of any views or sunlight, but the location put me in the middle of so much cultural activity. Just a short walk away were Lincoln Center, Carnegie Hall, and all the Broadway theatres. The only autographs I sought and got were from African-American singers Eartha Kitt and Lena Horne. Ms. Kitt sat alone backstage at her 1978 Broadway musical show *Timbuktu*, a revision of *Kismet*, with her huge dog, maybe a Great Dane, seated nearby. Easy to talk to, she signed copies of her autobiographies *Thursday's Child* (1956) and *Alone with Me: A New Autobiography* (1976). For the second book she generously wrote, "To David my love!! Eartha Kitt 1978." I felt comfortable enough to give her in exchange an autographed copy of my book on Richard Wright. Lena Horne, backstage at her 1981 hit one-woman musical revue *Lena Horne: The Lady and Her Music*, was too busy greeting loud Long Island sorority sisters to pay me any mind but did autograph my British edition of *Lena* (1965), her book written with Richard Schickel. Much earlier, freshly graduated from high school, I got an autographed photo that Jayne Mansfield, a big-busted sexpot of an actress, gave me at the stage door of her 1955-56 show *Will Success Spoil Rock Hunter?* "To Dave. My very best. Jayne Mansfield." The unglamorous photo showed her in a baggy sweatshirt with a friendly smile. She was a nice, sweet woman with no airs.

Living so close to the Broadway theatre district I would often check out the Duffy Square half-price ticket booth and the active street scene between 52nd and 42nd Streets: lots of tourists looking up at the bright lights of billboards and the flashing news from the New York Times tower, but rarely if ever any celebrities. One evening I spotted the tap dancing brothers duo of Gregory and Maurice Hines, then starring in the Broadway revue *Eubie (1978)*, based on the 1920s music of Eubie Blake and Noble Sissle. The brothers were just hanging out on a street corner near a fire hydrant. I had seen the show and guessed they were getting fresh air before returning to the Ambassador Theatre. Because they were laughing and seemed approachable, I thanked them for their terrific show and hung out with them to absorb their bubbling effervescence. Gregory would go on to be a movie star and, sadly, die of cancer in 2003.

Just walking the streets I encountered many celebrities, especially on 57th Street. Sometimes I interacted, other times kept my distance to respect their privacy. I never asked for autographs. In the Marboro Bookstore near Carnegie Hall I saw Zero Mostel browsing. I admired him for his acting, especially in the 1964 Broadway production of *Fiddler on the Roof*, and for overcoming the corrosive witch hunt of the House Un-American Activities Committee, but I did not speak to him. Across the street was the barbershop where I got my haircuts. There I met the cabaret singer Bobby Short. He asked me who I was, and stupidly I said "Nobody." I could have said I was a professor at Medgar Evers College and on my salary could not afford to hear him at the Café Carlyle. Could he get me in without paying the steep cover charge? I said nothing beyond "Hello Bobby Short."

One evening I saw Woody Allen, notoriously private, walking with his friend and fellow actor Tony Roberts. I said nothing. Another time I stood at a urinal next to Bing Crosby. I said hello. What can you say to a celebrity who is peeing? I think I said something dumb like, "Fancy running into you here, Mr. Crosby," to which he replied, "Great minds run in the same channels." Profound. At an Off-Broadway performance of the 1972 censorship-smashing sex revue *Oh! Calcutta!* I saw Bob Hope standing in the lobby with friends. I did not want to say hello because I disagreed with his support for the Vietnam War. I should have realized that he was in fact supporting American troops wherever they might be sent, hardly a cause for criticism.

In the 1970s Broadway theatre tickets were relatively inexpensive, even orchestra seats, not like today's prices that can run well over one hundred dollars. For some show—I don't remember what—I was surprised to find my assigned orchestra seat was next to the famously bitchy, nasty actress Lauren Bacall. She was blocking me from reaching my seat while she talked to two young men in the row behind us, maybe her son Stephen from her marriage to Humphrey Bogart, and Sam, from her marriage to Jason Robards. I spoke to her politely. "Excuse me. I'd like to get to my seat." No answer. Again, but a bit more loudly, "Excuse me. Could I get to my seat?" Ms. Bacall whirled around, seemingly annoyed to have her conversation interrupted. "I'll move when I'm good and ready!" She moved, then continued talking about how good a set designer Tony Walton was for Broadway plays. At intermission many Bacall fans asked me to pass their programs for her to autograph. I thought of making the fans detour around me but I silently forwarded the many requests. This great star did not speak another word to me. I was a nobody.

At another theatre I spotted the very funny Catskills Borscht Belt master of one-liner jokes, Henny Youngman, and his wife. I said hello but did not throw back any of his wife jokes, like "Take my wife, please." They were happily married for many years despite countless jokes at her expense. I can hear him saying, "My wife asked me to take her some place she had never been before. So I took her to the kitchen." His jokes may have been politically incorrect but never nasty or delivered with obscenities. I thought obscene language was okay as long as the humor outweighed the questionable language, as with another Catskills stand-up comic, Buddy Hackett, or more recently, Richard Pryor.

While I'm thinking of New York's many show business people, I should mention Joseph Stein, the writer of *Fiddler on the Roof*, the smash hit musical on Broadway *in* 1964, starring Zero Mostel, later a successful film starring Topol in 1971. Joe Stein blended Sholem Aleichem's stories of Tevye and this milkman's poor Czarist Russian Jewish settlement struggling to survive, with music by Jerry Bock, lyrics by Sheldon Harnick. This magnificent writer was a member of my health club on the 300 West 57th Street block, just east of my building on the 400 block. He discovered me sitting by the side of the pool reading the 1934 novel *Call It Sleep* by Henry Roth. About Jewish immigrants on New York's Lower East Side, the book was largely ignored when first published, and rediscovered through Irving Howe's front page critique in *The New York Times Book Review*, October 25, 1964. Joe Stein asked me what I thought of the book, its setting and its characters speaking in immigrants' rough dialogue. He was thinking of writing a script for Hollywood based on it. I told him that in my opinion the novel might make a good film. I don't know if he wrote a script or chose not to.

In my very own building one tenant on the floor above mine was a young ballet dancer other male tenants nicknamed "Twinkle Toes." His good friend was the famous musical director of the Metropolitan Opera, James Levine. I sometimes rode the elevator with them as Mr. Levine admired my Yorkshire terrier. I never thought to ask this rather chubby, approachable, highly talented genius if I could get any free passes to some performance or dress rehearsal.

At a tennis players cocktail party I spotted Dustin Hoffman, but he soon disappeared. When the Media Educators Association screened his hilarious 1982 film *Tootsie*, he spoke about going into ladies rooms with his wife, cross-dressing as a woman to study feminine mannerisms in preparation for his role. His story was amusing enough not to be anticlimactic to the movie itself. If I were to rank living film actors by how versatile they were in their various roles, I would without hesitation choose Dustin Hoffman and Meryl Streep.

Another celebrity I encountered through tennis was Gordon Parks, the hugely gifted African-American photographer, artist, novelist, nonfiction writer, screenplay writer, film director, and cinematographer, in short an amazing Renaissance man, jack of all trades and master of all. This man, known to the public primarily for his 1971 film *Shaft*, was a good tennis player I met at the Vanderbilt courts over Grand Central Terminal. I most admired his 1963 autobiographical novel of a black boy growing up in racist Kansas and the1969 film based on the book, *The Learning Tree*. Regrettably, in the locker room we talked only about tennis.

64

In another essay I talk about visiting a nudist colony in South Jersey and partnering in a nude doubles game with another fine and prominent writer, Gay Talese. We prevailed against our opponents and the heat, although at one point I was sweating so much I had to ask, "Does anyone mind if I put my shirt back on?"

Rod Laver, the red-haired leftie from Australia, one of the all-time tennis greats, visited the courts where I played. He was there to promote a new racquet and to play a demonstration doubles set. Before that event he invited any players who wanted to rally a few strokes with him. This opportunity caught me by surprise: I had not had a chance to warm up. As I ran for a shot I felt my hamstring go. Hobbling, I refused to quit until I could get off one good return. Then, unimpressive though my shot was, I could say I hit with the great Rod Laver.

While doing research for my Durante book at the Billy Rose Collection in the Lincoln Center branch of the New York Public Library, I recognized another researcher as Tiny Tim who had what could be considered 15 minutes of fame, a very short period of recording and television fame. Born Herbert Khaury, Tiny Tim had long wavy rather feminine hair he kept brushing back from his eyes as his falsetto voice delivered such songs as the golden oldie "Tip Toe through the Tulips," made popular by Nick Lucas in the 1920s. I did not know what to say to him, so I said nothing. I couldn't ask, "Are you really as weird as you look?"

On October 29, 1979, at the grand opening of the renovated former Americana Hotel, on 7th *Avenue at 53rd Street, renamed* The Sheraton Centre, I met and asked the terrific arranger-conductor of so many Sinatra songs, Nelson Riddle, famously dour, if he had ever worked with Durante. He frowned, "You could never change a note. Durante always wanted everything the same exact way." Maybe that steadfast opposition to change came from the singing comedian's early years in vaudeville, where every city on the circuit got the same material.

Riding the M-11 bus down 9th Avenue from 57th Street to Abingdon Square on the edge of Greenwich Village I sat next to Ramsey Clark, former U.S. Attorney General under President

Johnson. I had a captive audience on a long ride to try to get a satisfactory answer to the burning question "Why did the United States feel it was important to get involved in a civil war in Vietnam?" "Why did we support unpopular governments in South Vietnam when the North Vietnam leader, Ho Chi Minh, was considered a hero for defeating the French?" Ramsay Clark's reply was that the older American advisors, like Robert McNamara, Secretary of Defense under Presidents Kennedy and Johnson, believed in the Domino Theory. If one Asian country fell to Communism, others would fall. I contended that Vietnamese nationalism would be stronger than the pull of China's Communism. We should not have considered Communism as monolithic. Mr. Clark was polite and clearly had never been a war hawk like McNamara, who later admitted in a book that his judgment was wrong.

On a trip to Philadelphia with my wife to visit friends we toured the Philadelphia Museum of Art. There I encountered Jack Kemp, former professional football player, former Republican Congressman from upstate New York, and Vice-Presidential running mate with Bob Dole in the 1996 Presidential race against sitting President Bill Clinton. We discussed art. I resisted the temptation to bring up politics.

Although I have the greatest regard for talent and genuine accomplishment, I suspect many of the most famous people need privacy, not to be on perpetual display for fans seeking autographs, selfie photos, or favors, but to be a nobody like me.

23

The Care and Management
of My Hair

When our writing group leader suggested the topic of "Hair," it seemed natural that all nine women would write about problems they had fixing their hair in a way that would be most pleasing to themselves, family and friends. Women take a lot of time fussing with their hair, often spending large sums of money for the skills of a hairdresser in fancy, so-called "beauty parlors." But what could I, the only man in the group, say about taking care of *my* hair? After some thought I wrote about the rock musical *Hair*, its social and political significance.

Later, I thought again about men's hair, especially men of my age, late seventies. Some men have no hair at all and look fine, even sexy, like Yul Brynner as the King of Siam in the Rodgers and Hammerstein musical *The King and I* or Michael Jordan soaring to the basketball hoop for the Chicago Bulls. They're not self-conscious like some men who seek camouflage in an ill-fitting toupee. My hairline has receded, no doubt about that. My once copious dark brown hair is now thin and gray, a bald spot noticeable near my crown when the barber holds up a mirror to ask if I like the haircut he has just given me. Each morning when I wake up and look in the bathroom mirror after washing my face and brushing my teeth I check to see if any hairs are sticking straight up or at a funny, undignified angle. If such is the case, I take a comb and straighten the out-of-place strands, and *voila*, my hair is ready for the full day without another glance.

As far as barbers go, I don't even think of going to my favorite barbershop until my short haircut has turned into visibly fuzzy hair crawling down my neck and over my ears. That seems to take about two months, though I don't keep track of the time.

When I do go for a haircut, I see Leo, a Sicilian-American barber who speaks only two words in English to me, "Hello. Short?" I answer "Yes." He nods his head and begins to cut and trim, the whole time talking in animated Sicilian dialect to Joe, his partner cutting hair in the next chair. I understand French, Spanish, a smidgen of German and Italian, but not one word of Sicilian. I think of Francis Ford Coppola's Godfather films but say nothing. There are no subtitles. I'm sure neither barber is going to make me an offer I cannot refuse. Behind the seats where customers wait their turn there is a large map of Sicily. Where was the famous Mafia town of Corleone? One day I'll look at the map more closely. When my haircut is finished, Leo no longer holds up a mirror. He smacks my head with a towel to remove loose hair and dusts my neck with powder. I get my coat and go to the cash register to pay. The price of a haircut went up some time ago from eleven dollars to twelve. I hand Leo a twenty and ask for five dollars change. I say "Thank you" when I could have said "*Grazie,*" to which his answer could have been "*Prego.*" Leo nods his white-haired head and replies with the internationally understood word, "Okay."

I slap on my Nike tennis cap, yellowed from years of sweat, and head out the barbershop door to the McDonald's across the street for an unhealthy lunch, then home. My wife inspected the barber's handiwork, haircut after haircut. "Turn around. Let me see the back." I turned around. She gave her approval. I'm good again until visibly fuzzy hair crawls down my neck and over my ears.

24

Hair

If any musical could claim status as an embodiment of the Age of Aquarius it's the rock musical *Hair*. It opened Off-Broadway in October 1967 at Joseph Papp's Public Theatre in Greenwich Village, the Village long a center of social and political protest. After its transfer to Broadway in April 1968, it ran for 1,750 performances and its anti-war message proliferated across the country, even into England and continental Europe. The show was a proud and defiant in-your-face statement of a youth culture's insistence on personal freedom—freedom from nagging conservative parents, freedom from three-piece business suits, freedom from stuffy Rotary Club language. Nudity and profanity struck at the prevailing culture and cursed the unnecessary Vietnam War. "Make love, not war" was the mantra that created a new brotherhood and a new sisterhood.

J. Edgar Hoover, the paranoid long-time director of the FBI, was determined to infiltrate and destroy the peace movement through the top secret COINTELPRO, a program to harass influential leaders, including the Rev. Martin Luther King, Jr., whom Hoover despised. Anyone who criticized Hoover's often-illegal maneuvers, including government officials, was met with planted false stories intended to discredit them. No President or Attorney General dared to remove

Hoover for fear that he had files of dirt on all of them—truths, half-truths and outright lies.

One group of eight brave anti-war protestors, not hippies with their long hair and love-ins, but mostly family people whose chief protests had involved invading draft offices and burning draft cards, conceived a plan to steal FBI documents that would convince skeptical Americans that they were being spied upon illegally by FBI agents under Hoover's direction. In March 1971, the Monday night of the heavyweight championship boxing match between the hugely popular draft dodger Muhammad Ali and the war supporter Joe Frazier, the group broke into an inadequately protected FBI office in Media, Pennsylvania, a sleepy town north of Philadelphia. What these burglars showed to *The Washington Post* and all Americans was the extent of FBI penetration of the country's private lives—illegal spying and harassment.

Oddly, given its carefully cultivated image of invulnerability, the FBI never caught any of the eight burglars despite Hoover's assigning 200 agents to scour the Philadelphia region.

Three months after the theft and release of these documents came Daniel Ellsberg's leaking of the more famous Pentagon Papers to *The New York Times* and *The Washington Post*. Then came the revelation of the truly sensational Watergate scandal that destroyed the Nixon Administration after Nixon's overwhelming reelection in 1972. Hoover had died earlier that year, May 2, 1972.

In 2014, what were American citizens to make of Edward Snowden's theft and dissemination of NSA documents? Was he a hero, a traitor, or both?

For the most current background information about the 1971 FBI break-in, given in great detail, fascinating and well-written, and a brief, much less definite opinion on Edward Snowden's actions, see the book by former *Washington Post* reporter Betty Medsger, *The Burglary: The Discovery of J. Edgar Hoover's Secret FBI*, published January 2014 by Alfred A. Knopf.

Hair, the rock musical, seen in our rear view mirror over forty years later, has long ceased to be shocking in its political and social context. Its musical inspiration for young people has been supplanted by rap, hip-hop and other forms of music. Still, the spirit of *Hair* is alive and well. It cannot be crushed in an admittedly imperfect democracy by Wall Street billionaires, political super PAC or NSA tapping of everyone's phones.

25

Shoes

So many images come to mind when I think about shoes, both joyous and sad. I see Fred Astaire gliding gracefully across the dance floor with Ginger Rogers in the black and white RKO films of the 1930s, giving audiences an escape from the Great Depression. I see Bill "Bojangles" Robinson's shoes tapping a rhythm with little Shirley Temple in *The Little Colonel* (1935) and the Nicholas Brothers not only tapping a jazz number but doing leg splits on descending stairs in the all-black *Stormy Weather* (1943).

I also, sadly, see a huge pile of children's shoes stacked up at the Holocaust Museum in Washington, D.C., symbolic of the million Jewish children murdered by the Nazis. On the evening news I see poor children of many impoverished countries not only in need of shoes but in dire need of food for their empty stomachs. In Charlie Chaplin's silent film *The Gold Rush* (1925) I see the Little Tramp so hungry he cooks his shoe with the intention of eating it. This fantasy, a brilliant pantomime by a film genius, brings laughter from the audience, but such hunger is no laughing matter in real lives' desperation.

Finally, I think of the Philipino politician and wife of Ferdinand Marcos, Imelda Marcos, and other rich ladies with their collections of hundreds of pairs of expensive designer shoes lined up neatly in walk-in closets, and I think of the multitude of people with no shoes at all.

26

Junk Food

Like most kids I knew in my small-town grade school in the 1940s, I enjoyed what now is called junk food. Frankie Welliver ran his general store all by himself, next to our Fifth Street Elementary School. He carried some of my favorite sugary stuff: Baby Ruth candy bars; Reese Peanut Butter Cups; Boyer's Mallo Cups, with their chocolate-covered whipped marshmallow crème centers; bags of Hershey Kisses and chocolate bars with or without almonds; Tasty Cake chocolate cupcakes, three to a package with oozing vanilla filling; Coca Cola in bottles that I could shake and use to spray my friends. And wax lips that could make you look weird, chewable after you try to get laughs by jumping at other kids.

Some candy contained prizes, like little whistles in Cracker Jacks. Topps Bubble Gum had a color card for a different major league baseball player in each pack, cards you could trade for others you felt were more valuable. Mallo Cups for a time had a card with one letter in its name, some rarer than others. When you collected all nine letters, "C" being the hardest to get, you could mail in the cards for a carton of the candy bars. I received a package of twelve bars, which I hid under my bed, and ate them all over two days, after school and just before dinner.

At Carter's Stationery a block away, I could buy a nickel foot-long hot dog and a root beer and check out the sexy tabloids with their photos of women caught in "love nest" raids, all with black boxes covering their eyes and private parts.

I knew that my mother cooked and baked all sorts of gourmet and healthy dishes that visitors admired, but for me this was like being force-fed spinach. "Eat! It's good for you," my mother would command. She could not understand why I was not hungry for dinner.

Whatever junk food I ate did not make me fat. I remained a skinny kid. My teeth, however, suffered from all the sugar, and my father complained about the dental bills.

Many years later, I still preferred junk food: pizza with pepperoni, Coke or Pepsi, hoagies stuffed with onions, hamburgers and hot dogs, all sorts of fruit pies, eggs with sausage. My waistline expanded. Then I got into gourmet food like my mother made, especially Greek, Turkish, and Italian—Mediterranean dishes—supplemented by red and white wines of the world. My waistline expanded more.

Today my stomach tells me not to ingest anything spicy. So pepperoni on pizza is out. Hot sauces in those little red bottles are out. Just the word "jalapeno" sends my stomach into defense mode. In Palm Springs, California, I was about to begin a tennis match. Hungry, I bit into a bagel with red specks of something. I thought I had swallowed angry fire ants. No amount of water could knock out the jalapenos. Some tennis stars eat bananas on court. Next time I'll try a banana. And in Chinese restaurants I'll avoid any item preceded by a red pepper symbol.

While I love a good steak, rare, with a glass of red wine, maybe a Pinot noir, and portobello mushrooms, I'll try to eat more baked fish, especially a marinated salmon fillet, supplemented by something green, like asparagus tips. As an appetizer, a simple salad would be satisfying: lettuce, tomato, cucumber, black olives, and feta cheese. For dessert or a late night snack, instead of a dish of ice cream swimming in triple sec or brandy, I'll go for yogurt, plain and unsweetened, just like my mother used to make. On the whole, however, I still crave a juicy rare hamburger with a slice of raw onion.

27

Letters from My Dog Gracie

Dear Dad,

I love you very much. But before I talk about all the wonderful things we do together that make me quiver with excitement, let me tell you the few things I wish you did do. When you are eating I wish you would feed me more of your chicken, more of your steak, more of your cheese, and not wait under I have to bark in protest of how long I have to wait between bites. Even after the barking you are too slow and I have to scratch your leg with my paw. Also, when 6 o'clock comes and I still don't have my dinner in my food bowl, that's not right!

Oh, okay. I love the walks—more about that in my next letter. I love going to bed with you at night and licking your face before settling down. I love that you lie down with me near my toy animal friends, stroking my back as I bite each one.

Your daughter,
Gracie

Dear Dad,

When you snap on my collar with my name and phone number on it and you show me my leash, I get so thrilled that we will be going for a walk. I'm expecially happy when instead of a short walk around the block we jump in the car and drive to my favorite park. There I can check my pee-mail on the flowers and weeds. I no longer try to smell the lampposts since you don't like that, but sometimes it's a special treat when you let me pull you to a tree and let me circle all around it sniffing from every angle.

As you know, I'm more joyful with people who tell me I'm cute and want to pet me than with other dogs. Some dogs just want to bark or jump on me. I'm cautious with big ones, and let's face it, most are much bigger than me. I will only go nose to nose and check out butts if the big dog's person has a firm grip on the leash and you, Dad, assure me it's not going to growl or snap at me. I would rather back away quietly, maybe even stand behind you, if there could be a problem. Mostly, I enjoy saying hello to friends I already know, like Rusty the miniature poodle and Toby the shih tzu. If it's safe to do so, you then unsnap my leash and let me exchange greetings.

"How was your week?" Rusty asked.

"Good. I smelled a few good trees by the tennis courts," I replied. "The last couple of days it rained so we just went around the block."

"Oh, that's why I didn't see you. My person brought me to the park wearing a little raincoat."

Toby came over to say hello while his person fed a bag of peanuts to the squirrels, calling some of them with his own squirrel sounds that I found interesting.

When I see friends and no dog barks at me, going to the park is a fine adventure and I look forward to each new visit.

Love,
Gracie

28

Letter to A Landlord
(Not Sent)

I lived for 13 and a half years renting a well-located but not so nice one bedroom apartment when I first came to New York in 1971 to accept a position as assistant professor of English at Medgar Evers College, a Brooklyn branch of CUNY. This is a letter of complaint I would have liked to send to my careless landlord about conditions in need of improvement.

Dear Mr. Siegel:

When I first moved to New York I was happy to find a one-bedroom apartment in the very heart of Manhattan. From 415 West 57th Street I could easily walk north to Lincoln Center, east to Carnegie Hall, and south to all the Broadway theatres.

What I did not expect was finding cockroaches crawling over my bed as I slept or scattering in the tiny kitchen when I turned on the light. They seemed to return more plentiful than before after you sent an exterminator. My own efforts seemed no better.

Worse than the roaches was the breakdown of the building's boiler on the coldest days of the winter. Calls to your office are unanswered for days or I get a promise that the boiler will be fixed as soon as parts arrive. How soon is "soon"? Do I have to file a complaint with the Housing Authority every time this happens? I should not have to turn on my gas stove and use pots of boiling water to create steam. I should not have to wear every bit of clothes I own to keep warm and I should not have to buy an electric blanket so I can sleep without turning blue.

Where you live, do you have to deal with such problems? I think not. Slum conditions we see on television are much worse, but for the location and the rents we tenants pay it's not unreasonable to ask for and receive better services than we are now getting. Maybe start with buying a new boiler.

Sincerely,
David Bakish
Apt. 4-D

29

Falling

Once upon a time, in what seems a galaxy far away, I was a dashing, handsome young man, a bachelor living in magical Manhattan. I was limber of limb, able to leap down stairwells to catch the closing doors of a subway train, or run back for a tennis ball hit over my head. Today I must hold tightly onto the railing and settle for catching the next train. In tennis I have fallen hard going back for a lob, knowing it's safer to concede the point rather than trust that my worn knees will cooperate. In any case, I tried to remain optimistic as I grew into my eighties, moving more carefully in motions that were once automatic, like stepping down from a higher than expected curb. "Slow down and live!" I tell myself. *Zei gezunt!* Be healthy!

I think of the classic song of growing old, "September Song," Maxwell Anderson's words set to Kurt Weill's music, composed in 1938, the year after I was born. In the hands of its first performer, Walter Huston, and much later sung with heartfelt emotion by my favorite old man, Jimmy Durante in a 1963 recording, the song was a tearjerker of wistfully bemoaning lost youth, the days of life moving inexorably from September to December, our abilities withering like the autumn leaves.

As a young man unafraid of falling, I never thought of injury, breaking healthy bones, or dying. When I fell, I just got up again, as simple as that, like some pratfall in a slapstick vaudeville or silent movie routine.

Always a fan of musical chestnuts, the once-golden oldies, just the idea of "falling" brought to mind such songs as "Falling in Love with Love," by Rodgers and Hart, and "Falling Leaves," by Mack Davis and Frankie Carle. I especially like "When I Fall in Love (It Will Be Forever)," by Edward Heyman and Victor Young. When I hear that sung by Doris Day or Nat King Cole I think how my marriage to Linda had been an enduring one. On the other hand, the one song I once tried very hard to get out of my head instead of playing over and over in my sleep was the Academy Award winning song from the 1969 film *Butch Cassidy and the Sundance Kid*, "Raindrops Keep Falling on My Head," by Hal David and Burt Bachrach. After a time that song became "Shoes Keep Falling on My Head."

In short, today I may fall for you, but don't you fall for me. We old-timers might be too frail to do anything except call 911.

30

Commitments of a Would-Be Free Spirit

If you want to remain a free spirit, how many commitments do you have room for? You can be in love and committed to another person. You can be committed to your career. You can be so involved with your ideals that you are committed to a cause, like helping fight world hunger by volunteering your services to a do-good charitable group or by making regular financial contributions. You can feel so strongly about the political direction of your country that you will work for the election of people who share your opinions and try to keep those opposed out of office.

If any of the commitments you make intrude unreasonably upon the freedom you feel you must have, can you extricate yourself? From a relationship, even a marriage? From a career if an alternative presents itself? From a charitable organization? From a political party?

These are all admirable commitments, and exiting from any one of them could be emotionally, financially, or legally complicated. But it can be done to restore more of your free spirit.

But what about darker commitments? You will want to avoid crazy temptations that can lead to involuntary commitments. Like going bananas and being committed to a mental institution. Maybe backing out of a Mafia commitment and having to go into hiding, or testifying at a criminal trial and having to enter the federal witness protection program when you had a commitment of *omerta*, the underworld code of honor to remain silent and not cooperate with the cops. Maybe robbing a bank and, relieved you didn't get shot, seeing yourself in a hoodie and dark glasses shown on all local TV stations—in New York City that would mean ABC, NBC, CBS, Fox, WPIX, and WWOR. Publicity is great if it's free and leads to something good. This is not good.

On the brighter side of darkness, however, you could commit yourself to writing a book while involuntarily committed to a long prison term. I have a friend and former college colleague who did just that: he took part in a bank robbery and wrote an autobiographical novel with all the free time he had in prison. The well-established author Norman Mailer helped him get into a writing program at Harvard and find a major publisher. Then he landed a tenured college English position but never wrote another book.

Wanting to be a free spirit, make sure you don't break any laws that could take away your freedom. If you are like that early American free spirit Henry David Thoreau, you might not mind spending a night in jail for refusal to pay taxes.. Anything more than that, watch your ass and get a good lawyer.

31

Bike Riding

These days when I fall down and no harm done—no broken bones, sprained back, twisted ankle—I feel lucky. As a geriatric holding back bodily decay, I recall all the spills of youth. I never injured myself enough to need crutches, nothing more than iodine and Band-Aid.

I especially recall all the bike trips up and down Eastern Pennsylvania mountains. Uphill my muscular short legs had me zig-zagging with a single-gear old bike someone had abandoned, not a fancy ten-speed wonder. Downhill I stood up to apply brakes that I hoped would slow me down just a little, and that I would not hit any stones or gravel that would fling me off. I had no helmet. No one I knew in those days (1954) even knew of bike helmets.

With neighborhood boys I tried for a Boy Scout cycling merit badge. We completed six 25-mile trips and just needed one 50-mile trip for the badge. The new school year began and we never completed that last requirement. I think we should have received credit for maneuvering steep mountain roads. Midwestern states have vast flat spaces, a much easier ride.

The one time the chain on my bike snapped it was close to home, on level ground and at a slow enough speed that I was able to jump off. Not knowing how to fix the chain I kept the bike in our family's garage. When my Uncle Marco came to visit my parents with his wife, my father's sister, this founder of a garment industry skillfully and easily fixed the chain without being asked. In his native Turkey he had worked as a mechanic. He enjoyed fixing things. In America he often took pleasure in fixing sewing machines in his factory when hired mechanics could have done the work.

After finishing high school I didn't do any more bike riding until 1957 on a weekend train trip to Amsterdam from a summer course in conversational French at the Sorbonne. I loved that Dutch city for its art galleries, canals, and delightful biking on flat surfaces with two fellow students, both adventurous young American women. Car traffic was civilized, even polite, considerate of the many bicycles, not crazy like the kamikaze drivers hell-bent on the traffic circles I witnessed later that summer in Rome.

The next time I did any biking was on a summer trip in the early 1970s, visiting a Parisian friend vacationing with her family on the picturesque island of Brehat, off the coast of Brittany. There the hills were small. I lost excess weight, ate like the family, with small portions and no snacks, but with much wine and cognac.

After retiring in 1999, my wife, dog and I spent eleven winters in the much steeper mountainous roads in and near Tucson, Arizona. My knees were worn by meniscus problems and I was content to watch world-class bike riders competing in the Tour de Tucson, all wearing skin-tight spandex, helmets, and riding fancy expensive bikes with side view mirrors. Long before this, in the mid-1970s, my future wife, Linda, impressively rode a bike (minus helmet) from New York City's Greenwich Village to Montauk, the eastern tip of Long Island, 117 miles each way if you stuck to the highway. This before multiple sclerosis had sapped her energy and affected her balance (sometime earlier than our 1988 introduction to each other).

Why didn't I think of getting a motorcycle? A Sorbonne student from Philadelphia had driven me around the narrow, hilly and sharp-curvy streets of Montmartre one rainy night that great summer in Paris. But I knew someone who got killed on a skidding Harley-Davidson so I skipped repeating that adventure. I had already challenged death my senior year of high school by driving my father's car at 120 miles per hour. I would take up a less dangerous sport, tennis. With bad knees I gave up singles for doubles.

Have I spent a cautious life avoiding most bodily risks, or have I been adventurous enough, unafraid and unconcerned with thoughts of injury or mortality? In 1964 I entered Communist East Berlin by myself via the subway and past machine-gun toting guards. If anything had happened, no one would have known where I was, not the American Embassy and, long before cell phones, not my family in America. The totalitarian guards confiscated my map of Berlin as "incorrect," my copy of the *International Herald Tribune* as "propaganda," and tried to confiscate a memorial brochure of West German postage stamps showing ten major Jewish synagogues in Berlin that the Nazis destroyed: *Die Judische Gemeinde Zu Berlin* (The Jewish Community of Berlin). I fought in my rudimentary college German to keep that brochure. Perhaps I risked getting arrested. The inspecting Communist official relented and sealed the brochure, marking it *"verboten,"* not to be delivered to anyone in their territory. I still have that memento of Nazi savagery and a brief instance of corrosive Communist oppression.

Driving my father's car at 120 miles per hour, negotiating mountain roads with an old bike I could barely control, and arguing with armed Communist guards were challenges I enjoyed, just enough danger to make an otherwise calm life a bit more exciting.

32

Collections

My fifth grade teacher, a grizzled, old-looking woman with a warm heart and a sense of humor, collected United States postal stamps. After school she ran a stamp collectors club. The few other students who began collecting were specializing, like our teacher, in U.S. stamps, learning in the process about our country's history—with its presidents, its landmarks, and its dead authors, composers, scientists, inventors and heroes. (You could not be on a U.S. stamp unless you were famous, dead, and approved by the postal service.) My collecting, like most everything else that interested me later in life, was more universal. I began collecting stamps from all over the world, learning how each country spelled its own name and learning some of each country's cultural aspects. I learned about the many parts of the still-cohesive British Empire and the French African countries. Stamps from Nazi Germany especially intrigued me, with Adolph Hitler himself displayed in heroic poses. My cousin in New York sent me stamps from South America, Europe, and sometimes Africa and Asia, from the many queries that came into the publisher's office where she was a secretary.

Eventually, I answered newspaper ads in *The New York Times* from stamp dealers. They sent me sheets of world stamps on approval.

I paid for those I wanted. I knew which U.S. stamps were rare, but I never knew the value of foreign stamps, nor did I care. Many of these stamps were more beautiful than those from the U.S.: butterflies, lions and elephants, dogs and cats, artworks from museums and tribes.

Years later I began a lifelong interest in collecting books and music recordings. As with stamps, I amassed books in many fields— novels, poetry, humor, biographies, histories, psychology, sociology, philosophy—and music that ranged from classical and jazz to show tunes, early popular personalities, and early rock and roll. I never paid any attention to what were considered bestsellers. If I was out of step with the crowd, so be it: I collected what interested me.

While collecting was a solitary activity, I did find a group of similar enthusiasts who met once a month in a Manhattan hotel banquet room to sell, buy or trade records and related items, like sheet music and jazz magazines. The conversations rarely got beyond collector talk, and a program involved someone threading a projector to show soundies, early Vitaphone shorts of jazz groups and personalities. Additionally, every summer there was a Record Bash, collectors from all over the country and overseas congregating at a New Jersey motel to ogle rare 78 rpm records and listen to them, making purchases and viewing jazz and big band film clips. Out of these experiences I made two good friendships, one a pharmacist from the Philadelphia area and the other the owner of what might have been the country's largest record store stock of pop and jazz 78s, right across from the Empire State Building on West 33rd Street.

As I did with postage stamps, I wanted to cover a broad field, not specializing, but in time I developed a special interest in the old-time vaudeville comedian who sang and played jazz piano, Jimmy Durante. I collected everything he ever did—recordings, radio and television programs, playbills of Broadway shows, ads for his nightclub appearances, tapes of his movies, lobby cards and posters, autographed photographs and publicity stills, plus much else. Then I wrote a book on the career of Durante that was a finalist for an ARSC Award (the Association of Recorded Sound Collections), with reviews that were impressed by the depth of information.

When I got married at age 52, this bachelor/collector discovered that his much younger wife was a good sport. She bought me more bookshelves, not realizing I would fill these and again have collectibles stacked two or three deep and piled on the floor. As reality set in, she made the very practical suggestion that I should become a drug addict. That way I would sell off my collection to finance my drug habit. The lady had a sense of humor.

When we took summer vacations driving to Boothbay Harbor, Maine, she navigated our car to every used bookstore and used record store that antiquarian guides said was worth investigating. Years later the internet came along. Collectors now had only to browse websites from their armchairs. The adventure of discovery was gone.

Today's young people who collect seem to be more interested in collecting people, busily "friending" hundreds of names for their internet Facebook page, people that they never try to get to know more intimately. The list remains just a competitive collection of strangers. Who can collect the most names, as in "My list is bigger than yours."

I gave what I thought was a significant number of videotapes to a Catholic nursing home, history books to St. John's University, books and records to a thrift shop, and split fifty-fifty the income from the auction list sales of a widely known jazz record and book dealer in Connecticut. The space now liberated from what could, uncharitably, be called clutter, was hardly noticeable.

33

Friends - What and Who are They?

Sometimes when I feel depressed, I count my friends. How many do I have? Who are they? What do I expect from a friend? When my mother died and I was sitting *shiva* with my sister, mourning our loss, I thought about my mother's friends, past and present, and how she determined who her friends would be. My mother took time to develop a sense of the character of a potential friend, the quality of the person, before committing her generous affection to them. What were my criteria?

Sitting in the dark in what had been our parents' house in small town Pennsylvania after lightning struck a transformer outside, I felt an emptiness, a longing. I called my wife back home in New York and we talked awhile. Then, on impulse, I phoned an old high school friend in Colorado whom I had not seen or heard from in many years. He remembered me, he remembered my mother. The voice from the past soothed my sadness. Clearly, we were still friends.

I felt the need to better define friendship, not from a dictionary, but from my gut. How did I choose friends? How many had I gained and lost over the years? Who had died and who had simply drifted away? Which relationships grew and which withered from lack of attention? What friendships ended with irreconcilable differences, like a marriage gone wrong? Did the people with whom I exchanged an annual holiday greeting count as friends? I would have been glad to have more contact with some of these people while other relationships worked more comfortably at a distance.

When I have a problem and want to discuss it at length, whom can I call without feeling that I'm intruding? Would I be willing to listen to that same friend's problems with as much caring as I hoped he or she would afford me?

My dearest friend as an adult was a fellow record collector who died in the summer of 2001, in his early 60's. In our time, we shared common interests, enjoyed listening to music together, and spent hours talking over the particulars, favorable and not, of our lives. We often visited and spent weekends together, looked forward to retirement when we would have more leisure and time to enjoy. He left behind a daughter just graduated from college and a wife who wanted to maintain some of the friendships she had enjoyed when they were a couple. But visits only made me feel his absence more keenly and it wasn't long before we stopped calling.

When acquaintances and neighbors who might be friends ask, "How are you?" what do they really want to know? Are they expecting a quick "Okay," in response to their polite concern? Would they be put off by a detailed response that might be less positive or cheerful?

I have a group of "tennis buddies" that I see almost weekly but with whom I have the most superficial of relationships. At my tennis club there was a member whose wife had serious health problems. If you asked him how she was doing, you could expect a half-hour dissertation, in great detail, about her symptoms and all of their doctor visits. After awhile, people learned not to ask and even made jokes about the lengthy answers.

Although I have been something of a loner most of my life, in high school I had a small group of friends I felt close to. We emerged from the cocoon of childhood together, sharing adolescent experiences and trying to understand the life and larger world that lay ahead. One of these boys was the friend I called forty years later when my mother passed away.

In the end, I guess the only true definition of friendship for me is different from the careful evaluation my mother employed. Friendship, I feel, is a felt experience, difficult to define. There are many disappointments along the way, but when it's real, I think I know it.

34

My Mother's Paintings

When my mother retired from running a garment factory with my father, she suddenly had more free time than she wanted. She still prepared three hot meals a day, sewed aprons to raise money for Hadassah and the Beth Israel Ladies Auxiliary, knitted tiny clothes for my sister's doll collection, and hosted the music club that featured decidedly amateur local performers. Something beyond this was her beginning interest in painting. The wife of a college professor taught an informal course on landscape and portrait painting. My mother enthusiastically joined with the understanding that she be allowed to supply her delicious cooking to all in attendance.

Over the years she produced many Grandma Moses type landscapes, not from the picturesque countryside surrounding our mountainous small Pennsylvania town, or from her childhood memories of a rustic Bulgarian village, but from pretty scenes in magazines like *Life* and *National Geographic*. Then she expanded her work into copying photographs of her children, my sister and me. These paintings filled the walls of her home, with those of her two children as young adults taking the honored place of display over the living room sofa, in a room our mother insisted be kept spotless and unoc-cupied, as though it were roped off in some museum. For guests only.

Why my mother never let her imagination roam free—not just copying—I'll never know. Maybe she lacked confidence in her cre-ative skills, afraid to break out of some restrictive circle of conformity.

Today I have none of these paintings. I didn't want any of them on my walls. In my first independent living quarters I had reproduc-tions of Picasso, Dali, Renoir, and Van Gogh. Later my walls con-tained copies of abstract art by lesser known artists and an occasional original drawn or painted by very talented friends. Eventually, with a larger condo, I surrounded my bachelor self with movie posters from early films of the old-time singing comedian Jimmy Durante, the subject of my third and most successful of my four books. These posters were supplemented by rare, autographed 1930s photographs of Durante, as well as jazz lithographs and, in my bedroom, two collages by Romare Bearden and behind the queen-size bed many Yorkshire Terrier sketches that I bought at dog shows.

When I got married, my wife showed great tolerance for all my chosen artwork as well as my massive collection of books and music recordings. She added only her well-travelled lithograph of a Munch nude, and, near the kitchen, hung the black and white wed-ding photo taken on July 2, 1989.

My sister valued our mother's paintings more than I and was glad to keep all her works that our mother had not already gifted to various friends. Meanwhile, in my mind's eye is the portrait of my mother that she never painted. That virtual painting will remain vividly and forever in my mind. It does not have to be hanging on my wall.

35

Men's Coffee

At the condominium where I've lived since 1984 there's a group of elderly men who met every week Monday through Friday at 9 a.m. for coffee and conversation. When I joined, the oldest was in his mid-nineties and I was the youngest by about fifteen years. Ten men crowded around a small bridge table. Three had the most years being in this informal group and claimed prime spaces on three sides. The fourth was up for grabs: the first to arrive.

The one with the most seniority was a retired police captain, tall, lanky, and full of stories from over forty or fifty years ago. He still worked out on the leisure club's treadmill every morning before the group met. He had the prime seat, his back to the indoor swimming pool, facing the card room and a view of the younger women passing by on their way to and from an exercise class in their revealing tights. "Nice ass!," he exclaimed appreciatively.

Opposite him sat a retired plumber. He used a walker but preserved whatever mobility he had by faithfully pedaling a stationary bicycle each morning after coffee, assisted by a young aide. In conversation he specialized in sarcastic comments, with a twinkle in his eye.

Between the two sat a retired CPA for a large clothing company with plants in the South. He looked asleep, hunched over his neatly folded copy of *The New York Times*, but roared loudly when someone said anything he could challenge in his overloud, hearing aid assisted voice. His favorite word of scorn was "schmuck!"

The fourth prime seat was taken most summer mornings by a retired dentist, proudly wearing his University of Pennsylvania polo shirt. He went to Florida for the winter, and when in New York was often at an apartment he rented on Manhattan's Upper East Side. Unlike most of the other men he was a Republican but too moderate and too intelligent to support the crazy 2016 Republican nominee and eventual 45th President, Donald J. Trump. In better health than the other men, he was a widower with the money to enjoy opera, concerts, and Broadway shows sometimes in the company of a girl-friend he rarely mentioned. He carried a photo of his wife, dead many years, on his Apple iPhone 6. At 9:30 he routinely checked his smart phone for the opening of the stock markets and announced to one and all whether the indicators were green or red.

The dentist's seat, which the accountant said is not really his since he's away half the year, was, in the dentist's absence, taken by a charming 90-plus year old Sephardic Jew who loved to hum lyrics of old American standard pop songs until the accountant told him to shut up. The Sephardic gentleman was thrilled that I joined the group because I liked the old songs and because he could carry on a brief conversation with me in Ladino, the Judeo-Spanish I picked up from my grandmother as a child. He was probably the sweetest man in the group, a retired construction engineer with no acerbic, nasty comments to make.

Squeezed into the table you could find a retired jewelry salesman who was still mentally sharp and the only man there who wanted to read my book of my life experiences, *Zero to Seventy-Five*.

You were likely to find, arriving late, a retired engineer who was probably the smartest one there. His wife, despite her ill health, ran a very fine writing group with me as the only man out of ten partici-pants. Together husband and wife regularly won bridge tournaments held in the leisure club.

Midway through the hour, summers only, when not in Florida, you would find a retired motorcycle cop. The other officer called him a provocateur who would say anything to get an argument started. In the 2016 presidential race this cop absorbed and regurgitated Trump's lies about his Democratic opponent Hillary Clinton and insults against almost every other person and group who dared to disagree with Trump's opaque views. I told him he's full of shit and called him Archie Bunker, the right-wing central character in Norman Lear's satiric TV sitcom *All in the Family*. But because the comments came with a smile and a wink, I just laughed and found him amusing (like Archie Bunker).

In the first year I attended, two members disappeared because of health problems, reappeared to great cheer, then faded again and died in hospice care. One was a real estate lawyer who was less depressed when he got a motorized scooter, and the other a liquor salesman who rarely spoke up.

Once a month everyone went to a local diner for a birthday breakfast. The "birthday boy" got his meal free. The accountant would begin with a toast, all glasses of orange juice raised high. At the end he calculated how much each of us owed. When well enough to participate, the quiet liquor salesman would take an excellent photo of the group with his Nikon camera. Many wore their military caps from service in World War II or the Korean War. Once some stranger left a fifty dollar bill at the cashier's register in honor of our war veterans.

At men's coffee, seated alone at the next table sat a semi-retired pharmacist who still worked one day a week. When he wanted to give his opinion he shouted louder than anyone else but no one listened because there was so much verbal flack flying, people busy talking across each other, sometimes on totally different topics. Why, you might ask, didn't someone think of moving the two tables together? Tradition?

How did I happen to join this colorful group of complainers, most of them specialists in a panoply of physical ailments, replete with stories of VA hospital treatment? When my wife suffered a serious infection of her lymph nodes after successful breast cancer surgery and had to undergo a repeat hospitalization followed by rehab at a facility far from home, I was stressed out. My writing group leader suggested I go join her husband at the men's coffee group.

This proved to be so much better than spending mornings alone—although our dog provided some comfort—that I continued attending long after my wife returned home, at least on mornings when I did not have a tennis game.

Oh yes, and one year after I began attending, my neighbor, formerly a financial advisor, joined, and mostly listened without much comment, not one word of financial advice.

I was no longer the newest kid on the block.

Today almost all of the men are gone, replaced by other colorful characters. A younger smart-ass, a psychologist, refers to this geriatric group hunched around a table as "God's waiting room."

36

13, My Lucky Number

As a Jew who was bar mitzvahed at age 13, I often wondered why 13 was considered an unlucky or bad luck number. I looked it up online. Some superstitious people believe it is unlucky because of Jesus' disciples to sit at the famous Last Supper. Judas Iscariot, who betrayed Jesus to the Romans, was the 13th and last disciple to sit at the table.

Much of the Christian anti-semitism through the centuries can be traced to Judas, with the unfortunate name sounding so close to the word "Jew." When the Roman emperor Constantine forced everyone under his rule to adopt the new religion of Christianity, the Catholic Church promulgated and perpetuated the huge Trump-size lie, the libel that all Jews in general should forever bear responsibility as Christ killers. The Church did nothing to denounce and remove this unreasonable black stain on history taught to Christian children until well into the 20th century.

In my building as in many others there is no 13th floor. I sometimes mischievously remind residents of the 14th floor that I encounter on the elevator that they are really living on the 13th floor. Most, I believe, would not mind if there were an actual numbered 13th floor.

Not more than mildly superstitious, I like the number 13 because technically under the laws of my Jewish religion, of which I am far from an expert, at this age I now was counted as a man, one of ten men needed for a minyan to start a synagogue service. It did not matter that I was not yet a grown man.

If one doesn't count my *bris*, ritual circumcision at the age of 8 days, something I thankfully don't remember, my bar mitzvah was the first important event of my life. My parents were very proud as my cracking voice spilled out the Hebrew prayers.

Much later my first serious long-term love affair was with a French Catholic woman I met in Paris who was 13 years older. Still later my second long-term affair was with a Catholic woman from Colombia, 13 years younger. And when I married it was to a Jewish woman in New York, 13 years younger, born the same year as my Colombian girlfriend.

My favorite TV channel continues to be the New York affiliate of PBS, Channel 13, with its wonderful educational and cultural programs, constantly under attack from right-wing extremists in Congress.

Finally and most importantly, I will continue to salute the flag of our democracy with its 13 stripes, and with my vote help protect the Constitution from threats like the Civil War, Jim Crow segregation laws, and dangerous would-be dictators like Donald Trump.

Postscript: If you're interested, look up the mystical meaning of the number of this chapter, 36, as it relates to the creation of the world.

37

Columbus Day

For as many years as I can remember, I have resisted any celebration of Columbus Day. Christopher Columbus, an Italian, sailed with the financial support of the Spanish monarchy, King Ferdinand and Queen Isabella. The mission, with three ships, was to find the best trade route to the riches of the Far East, including India.

Columbus went in exactly the opposite direction, west instead of east, and given credit by my grade school teachers in rural Pennsylvania and everywhere else for "discovering" America, I could not understand how anyone could be given credit for discovering a land already occupied. All across America there were tribes of people with functioning societies. A white man and his crew accepted the help of the residents, then treated them as inferior (non-Christian) human beings. The explorers shipped "savages" back to Spain to examine like some prize horses.

Over the centuries the white settlers made and broke treaties with each and every tribe of non-white residents the settlers labeled Indians. Had Columbus sailed in the right direction, the only people called Indians today would be residents of India.

At the same time Columbus was said to have discovered America, 1492, his Spanish sponsors were conducting the infamous Spanish Inquisition, forcing non-Christian citizens, Jews and Moors, to convert with sincerity, leave the country, or be burnt at the stake.

Both sides of my family were forced out of Spain. The Ottoman Empire, Muslims, welcomed the Jews where they lived for many centuries. In Turkey and Bulgaria my families spoke the local language as well as Ladino, Judeo-Spanish, and brought Ladino to America in the 1920s. Other Sephardim, Spanish Jews, settled in Middle Eastern countries where they lost their Spanish and spoke Arabic, Persian, or other languages of their adopted countries.

I never thought any large numbers of Americans might object to honoring Christopher Columbus to the point of taking down his statue at what has been Columbus Circle in the center of Manhattan. Does it make much difference after such a long time? I think it's more meaningful to take down monuments to the slave trade: monuments honoring the Generals and politicians who tried to preserve slavery and destroy the unity of the United States, and take down the shameful flying of the pro-slavery Confederate flag.

38

Random Acts of Kindness

On one of our summer trips my wife bought a button she loved and she tried to work its sentiment into the fabric of her life: "PRACTICE RANDOM ACTS OF KINDNESS." Observing her efforts to put that into practice, I tried to do the same.

This was not easy, given my upbringing as the spoiled only son of Sephardic (Spanish-Jewish) immigrants. I had trouble with empathy, with moving beyond a self-centered life. My underlying attitude was "What's in it for me?" Even my participation in Boy Scout activities leading to the rank of Eagle Scout, with the group's encouragement to do GOOD DEEDS each and every day, did not move me into the realm of altruism I was no Mother Theresa, Mahatma Gandhi, or Albert Schweitzer.

As details of the Holocaust became clearer and more horrible than I could have imagined, I began to pay more attention to the enormous injustices prevalent around the world past and present. I could not understand why Jews were hated and for centuries denied equal opportunities economically and socially, nor why Negroes from Africa were imported as slaves and treated as subhuman even after emancipation. I could not understand why Asians and Eastern Europeans were considered less desirable as immigrants to America than Western Europeans. It seemed obvious that every person on this small planet Earth deserved the same respect, dignity, a liberal education, and livable wages in non-oppressive systems of government that balanced capitalistic business opportunities with a socialistic safety net for those in need. But did this new awareness turn me into an active crusader for justice? No, though I did vote for the more compassionate Democratic Party candidates in every election, and contribute a few dollars to charitable do-good organizations.

My inaction, crying impotently in front of a TV set over the many tragic events at home and abroad, rather than participating in organized social and political movements, did nothing to advance any form of justice. Embarrassing to say, I continued to be self-centered and passive until I met Chaquira, my first dog, introduced to me by my Colombian girlfriend in 1976. A tiny Yorkshire terrier with childlike and lifelong needs, she moved me to acts of kindness toward her, then other dogs, and eventually people. When we split years later I was allowed to keep Chaquira.. Had I had children, I might have experienced a similar or higher level of caring.

Perhaps I was not so lacking in empathy. As I look more closely at the scope of my life, I see that in my many years of teaching I helped thousands of mostly first generation college students, many of them immigrants, to improve their writing and analytical skills, important steps toward achieving their life goals. Outside the classroom, my personal life told another less empathetic story. A little dog made a big difference.

39

Seeking the Whole Person

It was the spring semester of college in 1971. A Japanese exchange student was dependably cheerful every day and one of the best in my English class, speaking and writing perfect English. She let it be known that her father was a translator of Norman Vincent Peale's famous book *The Power of Positive Thinking* (1952), billed as "a practical guide to mastering the problems of everyday living." This self-help guide, an international bestseller, was translated into 15 languages and sold more than 7 million copies. I had not read it and even felt contemptuous of such a self-help book, a thought I did not communicate to my student.

I was not interested in discovering anything else about this or any other student's background. I was following the pedagogical approach I had witnessed in my many years of higher education. The professors were concerned only with classroom performance, not the whole person. It was like the literary school once referred to as the New Criticism: you examine a work for its own merits, separated from the life of the author, the latter approach known as Biographical Criticism. My preference was for Biographical Criticism, but, ironically, in my many years of teaching, through my retirement in 1999,

I employed something like the New Criticism, looking at the work of my students out of the context of their lives.

In my personal life I looked at every date as a night's adventure, not interested in the woman's personal life. The result was greater distance and less chance that I would meet someone who might be a life partner. I remained a bachelor until I was 52. I was reasonably happy but often lonely. I'm not sure how I opened up more to see the whole person but it might have happened when I met Linda. At first I saw only an attractive and intelligent woman thirteen years my junior. We had a first date dinner at a romantic restaurant she chose. There I told her about the death of my beloved dog, with tears in my eyes and my voice choking. She understood my pain and told me of the death of her cats.

This emotional beginning was an opening to exposing and exploring our separate lives that were now coming together in a deeper relationship than any I had experienced before. In the process, I was slowly becoming less self-centered and less superficial. Linda had had some difficulties in her life. She'd had a previous marriage to a psychologist, had worked to support him in his studies, but then he had abandoned their relationship rather than support her education. This marriage took her far afield from her religious roots.

My falling in love with Linda, and with a Yorkshire Terrier that we both loved, resulted in my placing the welfare of Linda and our dog above my own welfare. The rewards of giving emotionally became, to my surprise, deeper than those of taking.

We were so compatible while in some ways so different. We both enjoyed film comedies like those of Nora Ephron's *Sleepless in Seattle*; Rob Reiner's *When Harry Met Sally ...*, screenplay by Nora Ephron; Billy Crystal's *Forget Paris*; Norman Jewison's *Moonstruck*; Lasse Hallstrom's *My Life as a Dog*; Peter Yates' *Breaking Away*, with terrific screenplay by Steve Tesich. As English majors we appreciated good screenplays. Not that we always agreed. Linda was enthusiastic about Louis Malle's *My Dinner with Andre* while I thought the only way I would ever want to watch two men eating dinner for almost two hours would be if I were included in the eating, drinking, and conversation. I enjoyed World War II movies like *The Longest Day* and *The Dirty Dozen*. Linda disliked war movies and excessive violence.

Linda had a gentle sense of humor, like Nora Ephron's, and a very calm temperament. I had a more raucous sense of humor, more like Mel Brooks' in his *Blazing Saddles* movie, and a temperament that could go suddenly from laughter to anger. The French would say *Vive la différence!* We learned to live with our differences, though Linda sometimes caught me muttering to myself after some upsetting news story, writing imaginary letters in my head like a character in Saul Bellow's *Herzog* (novel, 1964). In the midst of a fit of my bad temper our dog would roll over on her back to implore both of us to rub her belly. We laughed and good humor returned before more than a few minutes had passed.

When in later years Linda's health problems became more serious, our love, understanding, and years of compatibility made what could have become a damaged marriage all the deeper. In each other we saw the whole person. We liked what we saw.

40

Linda's Prayer

Written by Linda after her diagnosis with breast cancer

Today is _____ the _____ of _____, 20__, a new day.
This is my prayer.

Before even I open my eyes, there is pain. Sometimes it feels like more than I can bear. I yearn for the time when I was comfortable, happy in my body. When I could move and stretch and rest with ease and pleasure. But pain is my companion now, and before I can greet the day I take its measure and prepare myself to rise,

I can still move. For this, I am grateful.

I pray that the pain will be bearable today, that it may diminish and even disappear, that I can be restored to a sense of well-being and physical ease. I ask for this miracle to be granted without cost, without additional suffering or sorrow.

Today the sun may be shining, or it may be cloudy and grey. It may be cold, windy, it may be raining or snowing; today might be hot and humid. I live in a temperate zone where the weather changes frequently and can sometimes be extreme and challenging. May it always seem precious to me, a manifestation of nature in the canyons of brick and glass where I live, which is my home. Today, may it not be a source of pain, of hardship or sorrow.

May I be able to do useful things today.

May I be able to do for others today.

May I find meaning and satisfaction in the things I am able to do today.

May I find pleasure in life today, perhaps even beauty.

May this world move one small step toward peace and brotherhood today, one small step away from violence and hatred, terror and need. I think there will always be evil and catastrophe in our world; may they be balanced with kindness and compassion today.

41

Linda

(February 15, 1950-January 1, 2018)

Linda was my first and only wife, the brightly shining light of my life. She had been married before and divorced. I'm not sure I can do justice to her life, especially the many years of her childhood, adult life and first marriage, but I will try.

After her death I discovered many documents she left behind: school and college report cards, letters from and to family and friends, original poems, an unfinished story about our dog, essays and an exam blue book from a college literature course, certificates of excellence, photographs from childhood and up. There's much more primary material for me to absorb, mostly kept to herself. Perhaps not so strange there is not one photo of her first husband despite thirteen years of marriage. There are also no love letters, either to her first husband or to me. Linda and I did, however, exchange the most loving and sometimes humorous greeting cards for all occasions. I kept two shoe boxes full of cards we sent to each other. Ever thoughtful and loving, her cards spoke not only for her sentiments but also what she imagined to be the nose-licking sentiments of our dogs, whether Corey or Gracie.

Where to begin?

Linda's birth certificate shows she was born February 15, 1950 at 6:20 A.M. in Beth Israel Hospital, Manhattan, birth weight not given, daughter of Jack Kaplan and Betty Gittleman, living at 60 Hester Street (on the Lower East Side). Her father's business was given to be a salesman of dry goods. Linda was by far the youngest of four children, an unplanned pregnancy after the births of Phyllis, Joyce, and Milton. Jack was 43 at the time and Betty 39. As was the custom she was not given a middle name. The certificate does not give the baby girl's religion, Jewish, just that she was white.

Among Linda's files are many mostly undated baby photos. One shows her smiling at age 6 1/2 months. There are also photos of her with her much older brother, Milton. She adored him. An excellent athlete as well as very bright, Milton taught Linda how to play baseball, while he starred on his high school basketball team and played baseball. Linda kept her baseball glove long after she could no longer play the sport. It hangs today on my hat rack next to my Mets baseball caps. She was a Yankee fan, though she did not follow the team closely.

Linda showed her superior intelligence early, in all subjects. There's a child's crayon drawn card that reads "Happy Father's Day Daddy. Love, Linda." The card has twenty valentine hearts, red against a blue background. Inside and on the back is a tree, underneath the tree four yellow flower bushes and a bright yellow sun shining overhead.

There was a shadow on Linda's formative years. Her father died on February 17, 1956, two days after his young daughter's sixth birthday, from heart problems. Linda told me how her father would go to the Saratoga Springs Racetrack during the racing season with two suitcases, one full of clothes and the second empty. An excellent poker player, he would return home with one suitcase filled with dirty clothes and the second filled with money he had won. I don't recall any other stories Linda might have told about her father.

Linda's grade school years were spent at the orthodox Yeshiva Rabbi Joseph Konvitz, East Side Torah Center. There she excelled in Hebrew, English, and citizenship with certificates awarded. She rebelled against the discipline of the yeshiva. Even that early she showed an inquisitive mind, asking her teachers many questions when they preferred that she learn the official religious teachings and to question less. Her second grade teacher, Mrs. S, Feinstein, filled out a progress report for general studies, meaning not including religious study. Linda's grades ranged from excellent to very good . The teacher's comment for the first quarter reads, "The only fault that I can possibly find with Linda is that she reads too quickly." The second quarter comments, "Linda is reading much slower now. She must learn to remember to bring back papers when she is told she should. She is doing wonderful work." Comments for the last two quarters simply note that Linda is an excellent student. It was noted that Linda was absent 15 times, 0 times late, and promoted to the third grade.

The fifth grade report card shows Linda's grades good but not excellent. Either the teacher was a grouch or Linda's rebelliousness was increasing. The teacher, named Miss Kaplan, remarked on the first quarter report that "Linda's class attitude needs to be improved." For the second quarter the teacher's comment reads, " Linda's Reading and Literature grade was lowered one letter because she failed to hand in a book report. Her class behavior is very poor." For the third quarter, "Linda is capable of doing better work, but she possesses a careless and unconcerned attitude." Improvement is noted for the fourth quarter.

After grade school Linda convinced her mother to allow her to switch to a public high school. Seward High School was a breath of fresh air. No longer constrained by the tight discipline of orthodox dogma, she made new friends. Her newly found freedom expressed itself partly in her beginning to smoke cigarettes with friends from the Lower East Side, especially with lifelong friends Ellen Benson and Arlene Katz. The three were once faced with a flasher on the subway who exposed himself. Unfazed they remarked, "Oh! It looks like a penis but so much smaller."

Students thought she looked Chinese and included her in a gang called The Imperial Dragons. This bright gang member at Seward was awarded several certificates of honor "For Excellence in

Scholarship." Her graduation diploma for the academic course of study is dated June 1968, when she was awarded an Arista Certificate for excellence in scholarship, service and character. A bright gang member with character? Each year, grades 9 to 12, Linda showed her brilliance in the annual standardized Iowa Tests of Educational Development by achieving a composite score of just under 99%., when the average rank was 50%.

Perhaps because of her very high grades Linda was offered a scholarship to the very prestigious seven sisters Radcliffe College, attached to Harvard University. Her mother would not let her go. Betty felt the need for her youngest daughter's help, with husband gone and three other children grown, married and leading their own lives. "Go to Brooklyn College. What's the difference? Radcliffe, or Brooklyn College?" Linda did enroll at Brooklyn College for night classes and helped her brother Milton with his garment business, as his heart trouble began. She hated the college and thought women went there to find a husband, getting "an M.R.S. Degree."

At some point, anxious to get out from her mother's domination, Linda married her much older psychology teacher, Mark Balsam, and changed her name from Kaplan to her husband's name. She wore sexy clothes, showing herself to be a modern young woman. She related how she arrived in shul one day with a mini-skirt. Her mother's friend seated next to her in the women's segregated section remarked to Betty Kaplan, "Look at that girl! How she's dressed! What a *shanda* (sin)." To which Linda's mother replied, "That's my daughter."

There's nothing in Linda's papers about her marriage to Mark Balsam, not even a photo, and she rarely said anything about her first marriage that lasted thirteen years. Seemingly happy, Mark suddenly wanted out of the marriage. He had become radicalized by the far left New Alliance Party and had suggested to his wife that they have a baby to raise for his newly found political party. Linda, startled, told Mark something to the effect, "Are you crazy? I'm not going to raise a child for a political party. If that's why you want a baby, we're not going to make one." Linda was to the left of center, a life-long Democrat who worked for the George McGovern presidential campaign in the ill-fated 1972 election against sitting

President Richard M. Nixon. Mark's radical suggestion showed that they were growing apart. Linda had been healthy, not yet afflicted with multiple sclerosis. They had traveled to Europe, bicycled from their home in Greenwich Village to Montauk, the furthest eastern tip of Long Island, and biked to Cape Cod. Linda had the energy to do cross-country skiing and ice skating (though she broke an ankle on the ice).

By the time I met Linda, several years separated from Mark, who was the one wanting out of the marriage, she had a major loss of energy, plus stomach and bowel problems. She didn't have the stamina for long walks or, more ambitiously, the few tennis lessons I gave her. She was physically a much changed former athlete but with an enormously high mental capacity undimmed by her increasing challenges. Among other talents she had a photographic memory. She told me she once memorized the entire epic poem "Paradise Lost" by John Milton. Years later, married to me, she took a night course in medical terminology. One week she forgot to read the fifty pages assigned by the teacher. The class was told that after a ten-minute break they would be tested on the assigned content. In those ten minutes Linda leafed through the fifty pages and was the only one in the class to get a perfect "A" grade.

Linda helped her husband complete his studies while she completed a Bachelor of Arts degree at Hunter College, CUNY, as Linda Balsam, *summa cum laude*, graduating January 1975. She was so gifted that one professor remarked on a blue book exam for an English literature course that the essay was so well written that she, the professor, would not read it to the class for fear of discouraging the other students.

I cannot fill in the many blanks, the many unknowns of Linda's marriage to Mark, especially since she rarely wanted to say anything about him, and I did not press her for information she clearly did not want to provide. I did locate a book she and Mark had done together, a sweet flower child kind of book that she never showed me. As far as I know only two copies were created, one for each. The volume written in 1969, with colorful modern abstract art cover was entitled *Fire Music—a Gift of the sorceress: a collection of original poems by Linda Kaplan and photographs by Mark Balsam.* Most poems are original except a few, with proper credit given, including quotes from Kahill Gibran's *The Prophet, Ecclesiastics,* and Bob Dylan. The photos, mostly by Mark, are artful, all black and white. One photo Linda titled "Mark and me" was removed and is missing. (Incidentally, when Linda and I were married she preferred black and white photos over color, though both were taken.)

Divided into chapters on thick artists yellowish paper, Linda begins, "Chapter 1. A voice in the dark/ speaks of the past,/ and obscures completely/ the beauty of the night." Later there are photos of Bleecker Street, where Linda and Mark lived, guitar players in Washington Square, trees, some naked guy named Charley, a silhouette of Linda marked "me."

Among Linda's more rebellious poems in the volume, so neatly printed it could be considered calligraphy was this untitled work:

"So, I read a book
about some girl
who was a musical genius,
and her friend who idolized her
even though she walked out
on her all the time,
and sort of abused her in general.
and I went home and
got myself a $25 piano
and practiced being
brilliantly abusive
and thought that the whole world
was secretly admiring me
from behind corners;
wondering though
why I never got fan mail
or other signs of adulation,
and why no one wanted to talk

DAVID BAKISH

and why I felt lonely
even though I was
brilliant and witty and abusive."

Another of her poems in the same book:
"Now that the fare is thirty cents
and the union has its way,
I snuck me under a turnstile
and was caught by a cop today
Where are ya goin' ya smart-assed kid? That cop said to me.
I shrugged my shoulders then turned, bolted and made my get away.
Now that the unions have dumped all the commies and this is freedom's day,
Sneaking under the turnstiles is the only possible way."

The parents of Linda's close friend Ellen Benson, now an emergency room doctor with at least three kids adopted after a difficult divorce from an Armenian doctor, were also her close friends. Ravella Benson was an educator and political activist, her husband Ben Benson a courageous leader of a labor reform organization that fought organized crime infiltration of the teamsters union. He received many threats on his life but unexpectedly it was his wife who was killed, not by Mafioso but by someone who saw her withdraw money from her bank and followed her home.

If I had not gone to Israel for a bar mitzvah I would never have met Linda. We both worked for the City University of New York but CUNY employed thousands, faculty and staff. I was a professor at one of 26 campuses, Medgar Evers College in Brooklyn, and Linda then starting a new job at the CUNY Research Foundation in Manhattan. Sara Bichacho, wife of my paternal grandmother's nephew in Petah Tikva, Shlomo Bichacho, wanted me to meet a Jerusalem painter who had an aunt in New York.

It was, by strange coincidence that the matchmaker for Linda and me was Linda's mother-in-law, Lil Wexler, divorced from Mark's father, Jack Balsam. For a humorous storybook explanation of how a trip I took to Israel for a bar mitzvah in the summer of 1987 resulted in my meeting another employee of the City University of New York and married her, see a chapter of my last book, *Zero to Seventy-Five in 30 Snapshots* (2012). Basically, Lil thought a better match would be with her former daughter-in-law.

On our first date we went to a romantic Italian restaurant in the Village. I talked about my recently deceased dog and Linda mourned her dead cat.

Her landlady allowed cats but not dogs. I charmed her into allowing Linda to dog sit my two-year-old Yorkshire terrier Corey while I joined a group to tour Southeast Asia. I called Linda twice, once from Malaysia in December and on New Year's Eve from Bali, Indonesia. She was not home on the second call, spending the night with her brother and his family in Brooklyn. After a heartfelt phone conversation earlier in the month I wrote her a postcard. (Remember, this was way before cell phones and email for quick response.)

"Dear Linda,

It was great talking to you today. Sincerely wish you were here to make this beautiful place more beautiful still….It was also great to hear Corey bark and to get news of my Aunt Louise and mother. Keep well. Thinking of you every day.

Love, David."

My card was addressed to Linda Balsam at 23 Bedford Street in the Village, where she rented a ground floor studio apartment. Linda put the postcard on her fridge door. It had a photo of two chimps hugging each other. I drew an arrow to the sweet Linda chimp and another arrow to the squealing open-mouthed chimp that was me, making the sounds I liked since seeing Tarzan films as a kid and imitating sounds and movements of Cheetah. I liked to be the center of attention like Cheetah in the movies, always stealing scenes from Tarzan, Jane, and Boy.

In my absence Linda fell in love with my Yorkie Corey, Corey fell in love with Linda, and I missed both of them. When I returned I asked Linda on the phone if she would marry me, a question I never before put to any woman. Linda was startled and after a pause uttered two words, "Oh Shit!" I asked her if that was a "yes" or was that a "no"? She replied "yes."

My mother wondered if I knew Linda enough to propose marriage. Linda's family was very happy. Her sister Phyllis thought I looked like the actor Harrison Ford. Phyllis' daughter Jacqueline, a labor and delivery nurse at Hackensack Hospital, sent an engagement present with a note addressed to both of us, which Linda kept. "We are so overjoyed with the news of your engagement. It's wonderful that two great people like yourselves have each other to love." The Marc Chagall painting on the card was "The blue lovers." Linda's beloved brother-in-law, Harold, married to Linda's sister Joyce, took me aside. "You should know, David, that Linda is a beautiful and rare flower. Take good care of her." I promised Harold I would. The circumstances leading up to the wedding and the wedding itself are fully described in my *Zero to Seventy-Five* book, which Linda edited so skillfully.

At our wedding Linda and I passed out sheets with the lyrics of a very old song I thought would be a theme for the future of our marriage, Harry Woods' 1927 hit "Side by Side." These are the first two of its many verses we all sang, accompanied by the Paradise Swing Band.

"Oh, we ain't got a barrel of money,
Maybe we're ragged and funny
But we'll travel along
Singing a song
Side by side.

"Don't know what's comin' tomorrow
Maybe it's trouble and sorrow
But we'll travel the road
Sharing our load
Side by side.

Linda, Corey, and I were happy, even when stronger storm clouds appeared to affect Linda's health, and my too large a portion of my retirement funds got caught in a technology stocks collapse soon after my retirement. Harder times that came only intensified our love, making it ever deeper.

Before Linda's multiple sclerosis forced her retirement, she held several very responsible high positions as administrative assistant. Her vita sheet lists her as Coordinator of publications in the President's office, CUNY Research Foundation (1988-1992); Administrative coordinator in the Division of Clinical Psychology, Graduate Faculty, New School for Social Research(1985-1988); freelance work as a word processor for a legal journal and an architectural firm (1984-1985); Administrative secretary, NYU, with the Graduate School of Arts and Sciences, School of Law, and School of Social Work (1978-1984); patternmaker for her brother, Milton Kaplan (1975-1978).

A letter from Linda reached me on my Asian tour early in January 1988 informing me that she was just diagnosed with multiple sclerosis and it could be a serious challenge. I could walk away if I wanted. I responded that I would stick by her.

Linda's downward slide was slow at first with occasional exacerbations that came and went, relapsing with sometimes severe symptoms but then relaxing back to what was normal, called recurring and remitting multiple sclerosis. She had a bad episode in 1992, treated with prednisone by her neurologist Dr. Nancy Lewis while hospitalized for ten days at Columbia Presbyterian Hospital. That treatment did not work as Linda temporarily lost her walking ability. At the time we bought a studio apartment on East 9th Street so Linda could be near her work at the CUNY Research Foundation on lower 5th Avenue. After her position was eliminated we rented out the apartment until forced to sell by new co-op rules required the owner to be in residence one out of every three years.

During the many relatively good years we drove to Boothbay Harbor or Kennebunkport, Maine with Corey to explore the rugged coastline, visit quaint used bookstores, and eat lobsters and other seafood. When I took early retirement in 1999 at age 62, we bought a house in an age restricted Sun City community in Oro Valley,

Arizona, northwest of Tucson. Corey and I loved the desert and the Catalina Mountains but Linda missed New York despite the friends we made and the very liberal Jewish reform congregation we joined, *Ner Tamid* (Eternal Light).

When Linda's MS turned progressive in 2008, and in 2009 I needed surgery for prostate cancer at Memorial Sloan Kettering Hospital in New York, we had to begin thinking of being in one place instead of splitting the year. We held on until selling the Arizona house in 2010.

Once we were back year-round in New York Linda filled part of her time tutoring the son of Chinese parents, father from Hong Kong and mother from Taiwan. Joe Chen and Carol Wang ran Baybridge Szechuan Restaurant, working long hours seven days a week. Like everything she did, Linda gave teenager Brian Chen weekly lessons in vocabulary and American history. Linda initially refused to be paid but agreed to accept anything Carol Wang offered. Carol offered $35. "Okay," said Linda, never one to bargain over anything. As a result, Brian was accepted to prestigious Stuyvesant High School and later to NYU, his choice to stay close to home and major in computer science. In appreciation we would frequently receive free dinner delivery. Joe and Carol said they felt like Linda had become "family." When Linda died they came to the cemetery service with a beautiful bouquet of flowers.

In 2015 Linda had a lumpectomy for a virulent form of breast cancer known as triple negative. Jacqueline, husband Aron and I celebrated Linda's return home with festive "Welcome Home" balloons. We were briefly relieved, but a week later she had to return to the hospital to treat a post-surgery infection of a lymph node. From there she was transported to a rehab facility in Rockleigh, New Jersey, a much better rehab facility than the understaffed and much inferior Parker Jewish Institute for Health Care and Rehabilitation in Queens that Linda had to endure later. At Parker she often had to wait for hours to be changed, getting a urinary infection hard to shake, and she proclaimed the meals "dog food," in contrast to the better care and food at North Shore Hospital.

I can't list or even remember all the trips we took to various medical offices. These adventures became a blur in my mind, documented by many medical charts.

Eventually Linda lost her ability to walk. Then the really heavy blow! From a CAT scan at North Shore Hospital medical staff discovered a return of breast cancer, now in the bones, having spread through her whole body. She was moved by ambulance to hospice care at Calvary in the Bronx. After months there, three blood tests showed her hemoglobin level steady. As a result, the hospital's insurance required her to be reclassified sub-acute from acute. I was told I had to move her, and given a long list of other places. I chose Margaret Teitz in Jamaica Hills, Queens. It seemed less dreary than other places I inspected. The next blood test confirmed she should be reclassified back to acute. That's where she died on January 1, 2018, her niece Jacqueline holding her hand as she took her last breath.

Through many months Linda tried to find the right medicine that would dull her pain without dulling her brain. Many days I read to her chapters of a Laura Hillebrand book she liked, *Seabiscuit*, about the famous racing horse and its jockey. When I wasn't by her side we exchanged loving text messages every morning and night, plus cell phone calls when Linda felt strong enough to talk.

Jackie Friedland, Linda's nephew, son of her sister Joyce and Harold Friedland, recommended the Hebrew wording for Linda's tombstone, and I concurred with the same wording in English:

LINDA KAPLAN BAKISH
BELOVED WIFE
SISTER, AUNT, FRIEND
A GENTLE AND GIANT SOUL
LIVED WITH DEPTH AND LOVE

Going further, Jackie put together a 26-page collection of the fond memories of relatives and our dear rabbi friend, Sidney Solomon, who had married us, and with his wife Ruth befriended us. With tears in his eyes the rabbi led the funeral service.

The unpublished collection of essays, entitled "OUR LINDA,""
was for Harold's son a labor of profound love, a love that so many of
us shared. Jacqueline, named for Linda's father, Jack, adored Linda
from the very beginning and expressed the sentiment in her remarks,
"We all miss you terribly." Later she told me, "Linda left a big hole in
our lives." Like Jacqueline, her sister Raizie was impressed with Linda's
intelligence and individuality. "Never one to follow the herd, Linda
forged her own way—researching, questioning, learning and drawing
her own conclusions." Linda's nephew Velvy, brother of Jacqueline
and Raizie, recognized and appreciated his aunt's sense of humor and
her distinctive laugh. "She recognized the humor and absurdity in so
many things." Niece and daughter of Linda's brother Milton, Rebecca
Kaplan Strom, wrote," What I loved most about my Aunt Linda was
her eyes. They were filled with warmth and wisdom, just like my
dad's. When you looked into them you saw her kind and gentle soul."
Linda's nephew Yakov (Jackie) Friedland wrote from Jerusalem what
he understood to be Linda's legacy. His very wise words reminded
me, as a professor of English literature, of Polonius' advice to his son
Laertes as he prepared to return to his studies in France.

> This above all, to thine own self be true,
> And it must follow, as the night the day,
> Thou canst not then be false to any man.
> (*Hamlet*, Act I, scene iii)

Jackie writes, in words as wise as Shakespeare's, though not in
blank verse, that Linda taught us all to live as she did, looking to her
inner self for answers of how to live her life. He concludes, "All you
need to know about life and about living is there inside you. Listen.
Trust your intuition." I wish I were as wise and sensitive to life's challenges as Linda and Yakov.

Among the carefully weighed and heartfelt comments our friend
Rabbi Solomon made at the gravesite were these words:

Linda was the loving and devoted wife to David. They shared
their love and their lives for the last 28 years; sharing their hopes and
their dreams. They were always there for each other throughout the

wonderful years of their marriage. David's constant admiration for Linda's brilliance, her ability to tell jokes and, to be sure, her having graduated *summa cum laude* from Hunter College, never ceased to amaze him. And in this last most difficult period when verbal communication itself was so difficult, the visits and their quietly and lovingly holding hands and the frequent text messages with the many emojis, enabled them to share their deep and abiding love. David dedicated one of his books to Linda; it was but a small expression of his enormous love for and dedication to her.

Among her many papers I found an unfinished book Linda had secretly written about our dog she loved so much. Why this and so much else she wrote she chose to keep private I don't know. "'**The Story of Corey**' by Linda K. Bakish." After the title page the typed manuscript gives in large letters the words of a bumper sticker Linda saw on a car in the parking lot at Albertson's [supermarket], May 10, 2002:

DEAR GOD,
HELP ME BE THE PERSON
MY PET THINKS I AM.

The following page shows our Yorkshire terrier in her shoulder bag sown by Linda, with the words, "Corey Lives in our hearts." What comes next is a thinly disguised version of how Yorkie breeders in New Jersey whelped, raised, and either showed their dogs or sold the puppies that were not of show quality.

Chapter one of Linda's work-in-progress (nine pages typed double space) given the same title as the whole book, is followed by a second chapter called "Daniel" (seven pages). It's about me and my mourning the loss of my first Yorkie. Chapter three, "Corey," runs nine pages; chapter four, "Home," eight pages; chapter five untitled, is unfinished, only two pages. There are two single-spaced notes for how Linda intended to complete chapters five through eight. The last chapter, simply called that (eight pages), deals with the sadness of Corey's blindness and eventual end of her life The Linda character called Lauren is much moved by Corey's gradual weakening. The last day of the precious dog's life is described in emotional detail. At the head of this last chapter is a quotation from *Song of Solomon* 8:6.

> Set me as a seal upon thine heart,
> As a seal upon thine arm:
> For love is strong as death ...

At the end of the last chapter Linda placed the same photo as she used at the beginning, together with Corey's birth and death dates: May 22, 1986-January 18, 2002.

After Linda's coffin was lowered into the ground I fulfilled my wonderful wife's request to bury Corey's ashes with her. With the remains of our precious dog wrapped in her tiny winter coat, I dropped the container on top of the coffin. Linda and Corey were reunited. I saved the ashes of our later Yorkie, Gracie, to be buried with me when I should die and the two of us laid to rest next to Linda and Corey. I used to joke with Linda that I wanted a submarine periscope so my spirit could see the World Center spires. Then they came tumbling down on the terrorist attack of 9/11 (2001). So much for dark humor.

42

Matchmaking Again

Several months after my beloved wife Linda died, I was filled with a profound void in my now seemingly meaningless life and began to search for female companionship.

My close orthodox friend, the rabbi who performed the beautiful wedding ceremony for Linda and me on July 2, 1989, and did the burial service for Linda on January 2, 2018, together with his very warm-hearted wife, invited me to dinner at their house in the Long Island group of mostly orthodox communities known as "The Five Towns," including Woodmere.

Thinking that I might enjoy female company, they invited a widowed, middle-aged orthodox woman. As she entered, I noticed she was wearing a *sheitel*, a wig some orthodox married women wore to cover their short natural hair visible only to a husband It had long been clear that I was a liberal, largely non-practicing Jew. Lois sat at the large well-stocked dinner table to my right, facing the rabbi. When she spoke I had to ask, "Are you speaking to me?" I could not see her lips or any part of her face because the *sheitel*, like a *mechitza*, a partition separating men from women in religious services, blocked my view.

The conversation turned unexpectedly to the topic I had tried hard to avoid with Trump supporters, Israeli and American politics. Lois said she was accustomed to spending five months of each year in a place she had in Israel and liked the right-wing Likud Party leader Benjamin Netanyahu, friendly with President Donald Trump. On TV she enjoyed Fox News Trump apologist Sean Hannity. I stuck my finger in my mouth as if I was going to vomit. The rabbi's wife saw this and released a pained grimace or smile while the speaker remained oblivious. movie. I politely but insistently declined.

After that misfire these same friends tried again, this time a somewhat younger woman who seemed a dating possibility. She was a social worker with handicapped children, divorced twice, beautiful hair rapped around her waist long enough to have played Lady Godiva. The four of us enjoyed a nearby park at sunset and I drove Jane home, got her phone number, but never called her. Maybe the chemistry was not right.

A free first-year membership at Temple Beth El, a reform Jewish congregation in Great Neck, Long Island, was at first helpful in meeting people, but I did not renew for a second year. (Most emotional for me was the *Mi'she'Berach* prayer for healing. So many family and friends prayed that Linda would recover, including Christian friends with similar prayers.)

I signed up for a dating service. It was overload. My computer coughed out exactly 24 potential matches every single day. Ridiculous and mostly not appropriate. The computer did not restrict itself to women who fit my stated parameters. I got photos and profiles from women geographically far away and too old or too young. Aside from other statistics that the women and I provided in our listings, here's my summary of who I am and what I want:

"Widowed after loving marriage. Ph.D. in English literature, play a lot of tennis, like baseball, jazz, classical music, small dogs. Author of much-praised book on Jimmy Durante.

"Seek a warm-hearted, caring woman with a sense of humor, preferably Jewish. Absolutely no supporters of lying, con-man Trump."

Most women whose photos and profile attracted my attention were in their late 60's and early 70's, only two my age, both retired medical internists. Many women did not want any man over 70 or 75. Two Ph.D. psychologists liked me until I indicated that I did not have enough money to travel around the world and go to operas while paying the full freight. Others were willing to share expenses. A few women showed photos that must have been taken years ago and lied about their age. Sort of like Trump's incessant lies, "an alternate reality." Two women wanted to jump into bed just on the strength of intellectual phone conversations. Before even meeting in person, one wanted me to get a supply of Viagra (which my surgeon had prescribed) and was willing to share expenses. I got nervous and backed out, partly because I was afraid of how poorly I might perform after my prostate surgery and long period of involuntary abstinence, given my wife's medical condition. (As much as I slept around before marriage, I was always a faithful husband.) One wacky psychoanalyst thought smart men are sexy and wanted me to join her, not at her North Shore of Long Island estate, but at her second home in Montreal, Canada. When I suggested we share expenses, this still-practicing shrink dropped me, over the phone, like the proverbial hot potato. "No, I can't do that."

Occasionally I let my humor fly unrestrained. In response to a nice lady's listing that she was 79, in New York, Jewish, and other nice details, looking for men 69-103 within 50 miles of New York, NY, I emailed…

"Hi. I'm 104. Is that ok? I still have my own teeth (no newfangled implants) and walk without a cane or walker. Hear well in right ear, left ear more creative hearing, may need hearing aid soon. Eyes okay to drive at night."

No response and likely never read.

Most of the women I have met live "in the city," meaning Manhattan, highly educated and accomplished, with Ph.D. or medical degrees. They love the city for all its cultural treasures, not ever thinking of relocating to an outer borough with excellent housing at lower cost and less traffic chaos. (I well remember my own xenophobia, scorning the "outer boroughs," when I was young, single, and enjoying "the city" despite the cockroaches.)

I have Linda in my heart, as I told her, "for all eternity and beyond," but I have room for at least one more warm, caring companion, not a replica of Linda but a sweet, gracefully aging lady on the same wave length of compatibility. Maybe even with a sweet dog.

Jumping forward to November 2021, I met an attractive and sweet Jewish woman from Brooklyn only two years younger than I whose name by coincidence was also Linda. In her retirement from high school teaching, French and Italian, she enjoys substituting in elementary schools and loves the younger kids. On Saturdays she plays classical piano with a chamber music group. We both have a sense of humor and love dogs. We speak to dog walkers in the park and wish we were young enough and sprightly enough to share the love and responsibility of a little doggie. We both are a bit hard of hearing so our conversations can be humorous. "What did you say?" "Who shot who?" "No, it's who shot whom?" Linda cares about grammar and has a vocabulary that beats me in games of Scrabble. Oh yes, and I just got a hearing aid at age 86.

43

Appendix:
Three Photos of Linda

Milton Keynes UK
Ingram Content Group UK Ltd.
UKHW010241221123
432980UK00002B/242